A Style and Usage Guide to Writing about Music

Thomas Donahue

The Scarecrow Press, Inc.
Lanham, Maryland • Toronto • Plymouth, UK
2010

SCARECROW PRESS, INC.

Published in the United States of America
by Scarecrow Press, Inc.
A wholly owned subsidiary of
The Rowman & Littlefield Publishing Group, Inc.
4501 Forbes Boulevard, Suite 200, Lanham, Maryland 20706
www.scarecrowpress.com

Estover Road
Plymouth PL6 7PY
United Kingdom

British Library Cataloguing in Publication Information Available

Library of Congress Cataloging-in-Publication Data

Donahue, Thomas, 1953–
   A style and usage guide to writing about music / Thomas Donahue.
      p. cm.
   Includes bibliographical references and index.
   ISBN 978-0-8108-7431-2 (pbk. : alk. paper) — ISBN 978-0-8108-7432-9 (ebook)
   1. Musicology–Authorship–Style manuals. 2. Musical criticism–Authorship–Style manuals. 3. Academic writing. 4. Report writing. I. Title.
   ML3797.D76   2010
   808'.06678–dc22   2009051837

♾™ The paper used in this publication meets the minimum requirements of American National Standard for Information Sciences—Permanence of Paper for Printed Library Materials, ANSI/NISO Z39.48-1992.
Manufactured in the United States of America.

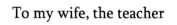

To my wife, the teacher

Contents

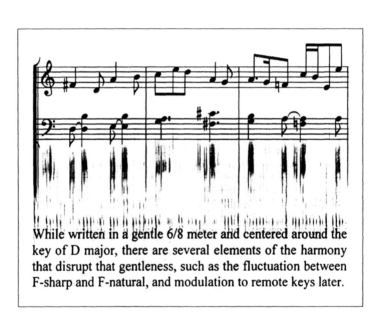

While written in a gentle 6/8 meter and centered around the key of D major, there are several elements of the harmony that disrupt that gentleness, such as the fluctuation between F-sharp and F-natural, and modulation to remote keys later.

Morphing Music by Jill Spaeth
Copyright © 2007 by Jill Spaeth. Used by permission.

Preface

A Style and Usage Guide to Writing about Music is meant to assist those who write about music communicate their ideas clearly and effectively. It presents a collection of guidelines that are designed to help express through the written word the special notations, terms, and concepts found in the discipline of music. The guidelines are not to be understood as strict rules to be blindly followed. Rather, they are recommendations that one should consider in the interest of clarity. It is expected that some of the guidelines may need "bending" in certain circumstances in order to meet the needs of the writer, given the flexible and ever-changing character of the English language, and because there are sometimes alternate but equally acceptable methods of expression. On the other hand, a degree of precision in formal writing has long-standing value. Ultimately the style that emanates from the use of these guidelines should be transparent enough—not drawing attention to itself—that a reader will get a clear sense of what the writer is trying to say. (It should be noted that "the writer" refers to the person using this book in the preparation of a work, while "the reader" is the person who will be reading that writer's work.)

There are several principles around which this guide is designed:

1. This book is based on United States English and so preference is given to anglicized terms and constructions. This also means that non-English words are governed by the rules of English.

2. Even though we are dealing with words on a page, format and syntax must take into account how words are pronounced.

3. Good writing takes precedence over musical jargon.

4. Problems in verbalizing musical conventions may be circumvented by rewording or reorganizing a sentence.

The present work is directed toward style and format. It is not meant to be a handbook on grammar, or on methods of researching and organizing material, or on the various modes of musical writing such as analysis, commentary, and criticism.

This guide is organized by topic and employs numbered sections or paragraphs. This format has been used for many years by other comprehensive style guides, notably *The Chicago Manual of Style* and the *United States Government Printing Office Style Manual*. I use it here because of its organizational value and claim no originality in its use.

The decision as to which guidelines should be included was based on my opinion about what details a writer would most likely encounter, as well as what were considered the most musically relevant topics. There was no attempt to be encyclopedic. The guidelines are a combination of widely used musical conventions, material gleaned from a review of many references, and my reactions to reading a variety of writing. Some of the guidelines are based on appropriate English usage, others on specific rationales, still others on what promotes readability. Some are admittedly arbitrary.

The examples given for the guidelines should be considered illustrative, not comprehensive. Likewise, not all exceptions have been noted. While I have tried to use mostly musically related examples, some examples are such classic illustrations of a guideline that not to include them would be considered a major omission, such as "in-val'-id" versus "in'-va-lid" to demonstrate how hyphenation changes with pronunciation. Unfortunately, it is almost impossible to document the originator of such examples because they have been repeated so many times and because the "genealogy" of the style guides—the trail of influence of one guide on others—is not easy to unravel. Again, I do not claim originality for such examples.

If the writer needs to alter or bypass a guideline, or invent a new format, it is always prudent to alert the reader and be consistent in its use. When deciding to use an unconventional style or format, the resulting sentence should contain—in the words of William Strunk Jr.—some "compensating merit"; that is, the unconventionality should be vastly overshadowed by the positive impact on the reader of the resulting sentence structure.

I wish to thank Jill Spaeth for her image entitled *Morphing Music*, which is a visual representation of that mysterious area between music and the written word. My thanks also to Gregory Crowell for reading the manuscript and making many valuable suggestions.

1

Names

1.1. Spelling and form. Names of persons may vary in two main respects: spelling and form. The spelling of a name may be as simple as the difference of one letter (Händel vs. Handel, Reinken vs. Reincken) or may be as complicated as the existence of multiple transliterations (Tchaikovsky, Tschaikowsky, Chaikovski, Chaykovsky, Čajkovskij, Czajkowski, etc.).

The form of a name relates to such things as:

1. initials: Carl Philipp Emanuel Bach *vs.* C. P. E. Bach; Amy Beach *vs.* Mrs. H. H. A. Beach;
2. variant names: Mendelssohn *vs.* Mendelssohn-Bartholdy; Mozart's middle name as Amadè, Amadeus, Gottlieb, or Theophilus;
3. name changes: Steven Demetre Georgiou *vs.* Cat Stevens *vs.* Yusuf Islam; Walter Carlos *vs.* Wendy Carlos;
4. nicknames: Bing Crosby *vs.* Harry Lillis Crosby; Duke Ellington *vs.* Edward Kennedy Ellington; and
5. pseudonyms: Wallingford Riegger *vs.* Gerald Wilfring Gore *vs.* John H. McCurdy *vs.* William Richards, etc.

Ultimately, the writer must select one spelling or one form of a personal name and live with it. One suggestion is to use the spelling or form given by an authoritative source such as a music dictionary, a biography, or an autograph of the person. If there is a rationale for using a particular spelling or form, inform the reader. Do not burden the reader with endless variants unless there is a reason to do so; for example, an essay on how Mozart signed his name, or on the transliteration of Russian names. Quoted material that deviates from one's selected usage could be indicated to the reader.

> Of Handel's method of composing, Smith wrote
> "Haendel [sic] was known to have . . ."

1

1.2. Correct spellings. Be careful to check the spelling of a person's name, particularly if there are no variant spellings.

> Elliott Carter, Eliot Fisk
> Emanuel Ax, Emmanuel Chabrier
> Aaron Copland, Stewart Copeland
> Jacqueline Du Pré, Marcel Dupré
> Alfred Mendelsohn, Felix Mendelssohn
> Christian Schubart, Franz Schubert
> William Schuman, Robert Schumann
> Randall Thompson, Virgil Thomson
> Wolfgang Zuckermann, Pinchas Zukerman

> Edvard Grieg, *not* Greig
> Franz Liszt, *not* Lizst
> Arnold Schoenberg, *not* Schönberg

1.3. Diacritical marks and special characters. Do not omit diacritical marks or special characters; this is equivalent to misspelling—or, more accurately, mispronouncing—a name. The German character ß (esszet) may be retained or anglicized to *ss*.

Béla Bartók	Gabriel Fauré
Léon Boëllmann	Leoš Janáček
Ignaz Bösendorfer	Zoltán Kodály
Aristide Cavaillé-Coll	Toshirō Mayuzumi
François Couperin	Per Nørgård
Antonín Dvořák	Camille Saint-Saëns
Sébastien Érard	Silvius Leopold Weiß (*or* Weiss)

1.4. Short form. Provide a person's full name at its first occurrence; thereafter a shortened form may be used, typically the last name alone. Non-English names with particles—*d'*, *de*, *du*, *la*, *le*, *van*, *von*, and so on—are included when a person's full name is given, but their inclusion varies with the short form or when listed alphabetically in an index. Some examples are given here; one may need to consult an expert in the respective language. While it is an acceptable practice to use just the last name, there may be circumstances in which the writer feels a more respectful form should be used, such as Maestro Hogwood for Christopher Hogwood, Professor Williams for Peter Williams, or

Miss von Stade for Frederica von Stade (as is found on her website). First names may be used under some circumstances, particularly for well-known persons such as Aretha (Franklin) and Elvis (Presley). (See also section 1.9.) Note that names such as d'Anglebert and d'Indy would have the *d* capitalized when the name starts a sentence, and would be alphabetized according to the letter after the *d'*.

Full name	Short name
Adam de la Halle	Adam
François Bédos de Celles	Bédos *or* Dom Bédos
Ludwig van Beethoven	Beethoven
Jean-Henri d'Anglebert	d'Angelbert
Norman Dello Joio	Dello Joio
Sir Edward Elgar	Elgar *or* Sir Edward
Manuel de Falla	Falla
Nicolas de Grigny	Grigny
Vincent d'Indy	d'Indy
Josquin Desprez	Josquin
Claude le Jeune	Le Jeune
Sir Andrew Lloyd Webber	Lloyd Webber
Guillaume de Machaut	Machaut
Camille Saint-Saëns	Saint-Saëns
Nicolai Rimsky-Korsakov	Rimsky-Korsakov
Jimmy Van Heusen	Van Heusen
Jacob van Vleck	Van Vleck
Ralph Vaughan Williams	Vaughan Williams

1.5. Birth and married names. A name change for a married woman may be written in several ways. One should determine the name under which the person is most known, how the person preferred her name to appear, or according to a documented form of the name. Those known by their married names may have their birth name included in parentheses with the designation "née." Use of both the birth and married names together may or may not include a hyphen.

Anna Magdalena Bach (née Wilcke)
Clara Schumann (née Wieck)
Amy Marcy Cheney Beach
Undine Smith Moore
Peggy Stuart-Coolidge

1.6. Plural. Form the plural of a name by adding *s*, or by adding *es* if the name ends in *s* or an S-related sound, such as *sh* or *z*. Do not use an apostrophe with an *s* ('s) to form the plural of a name. To avoid problems of appearance and pronunciation, try rewording the sentence.

> How many Bachs were organists?
> How many Strausses wrote waltzes?

> *not*
> the house where the Sessionses lived
> *but*
> the house where the Sessions family lived

1.7. Possessive. Form the possessive of a name by adding an apostrophe and an *s* regardless of the last letter in the name.

Sibelius's music	Françaix's style
Strauss's time	Boulez's compositions

1.8. Plural possessive. Form the possessive of plural names that end in *s* by adding only an apostrophe ("the Couperins' music"). Some plural possessives can get complicated, so it may be best to rewrite the sentence.

> *not*
> a collection of the Strausses' waltzes
> *but*
> a collection of waltzes by the Strauss family

1.9. Same name. Persons from the same family mentioned in the same essay need to be differentiated. Short of using the person's entire name at each mention, this may be done by first name alone, initials plus last name, or a combination of names and initials. Do not use single initials by themselves. If there is a well-known appellation, use that ("Johann the younger" for Johann Strauss Jr., "François *le grand*" for François Couperin, d. 1633). Occasionally, middle names are used—especially for the Bach family—which is acceptable if the names are well known and unambiguous. The use of the word "Bach" by itself usually assumes Johann Sebastian is meant, providing no other Bachs are mentioned. A particularly complicated example is "Johann Christoph Bach," which refers to several persons. For this name, each person would need to be differentiated in some way: year of birth, year of death, city of residence, occupation, relation to J. S. Bach, or place in a genealogical chart. Unrelated persons with the same name are differentiated similarly.

Bach   Anna Magdalena, Carl Philipp Emanuel,
            Johann Sebastian, Wilhelm Friedemann,
        or
        A. M. Bach, C. P. E. Bach, J. S. Bach, W. F. Bach
        or
        Magdalena, Emanuel, Sebastian, Friedemann

Scarlatti   Alessandro, Domenico, Francesco, Giuseppe
        or
        A. Scarlatti, D. Scarlatti, F. Scarlatti, G. Scarlatti
        not
        A., D., F., G.

Strauss   Eduard, Eduard L. M., Johann Jr., Johann M. E.,
            Johann Sr., Josef
        not
        E. Strauss, J. Strauss

The guitarist John Williams performed a piece by the
    composer John Williams.

1.10. Initials. When giving an initialized name in running text, use periods and spaces. Use hyphenated initials if the name is hyphenated. If only complete initials are used for a particular reason, periods may be omitted.

C. P. E. Bach, *not* C.P.E. Bach, *not* CPE Bach
M.-A. Charpentier (for Marc-Antoine)
The initials "JSB" on the manuscript probably refer to J. S. Bach.

1.11. Name suffixes. With the suffixes "Sr." and "Jr." commas are often used, but eliminating them sometimes looks less cluttered. If used, place them both before and after "Sr." and "Jr." With the suffixes "II" and "III" there are no commas. Use suffixes only when the full name is given; isolated last names do not have them.

Johann Strauss, Sr., was . . .
or
Johann Strauss Sr. was . . .

We heard Harry Connick Jr. in concert. Connick is . . .
Oscar Hammerstein II collaborated with many composers.
   Hammerstein was . . .

1.12. Adjectives. To create an adjective from a name, add a prefix or suffix such as *-like*, *quasi-*, or *-esque*. If the resulting term does not "read" well, try substituting another prefix or suffix. The most useful suffix is *ian* without a hyphen. If the name ends in *e*, *i* or *y*, use *an*; if it ends in *a*, *ea*, or *ia*, use *n*. Try not to alter the spelling of the original name; however, some names may require a change in the final one or two letters. Some names require the addition of an extra consonant in order to improve pronounceability. Consider rewriting the sentence to avoid such creations if the resulting term is unflattering or grotesque.

Bach	Bach-like, Bachian
Wagner	quasi-Wagner, Wagnerian
Copland	Coplandesque
Mozart	Mozartian *or sometimes* Mozartean
Varèse	Varèsean
Segovia	Segovian
Debussy	Debussyan *or* Debussian
Shaw	Shavian
Praetorius	Praetorian
Rameau	Rameauian *or* Rameauvian
Rodrigo	Rodrigonian

avoid

Ax-esque	Leich-like	quasi-Tosi
Hessian	Ianian	Khachaturianian

1.13. Isms. Occasionally it is useful to construct a term based on the doctrines, philosophy, or mannerisms of a person by adding the suffix *-ism* or *-isms*. This is most effective if it is used sparingly, if it is not confusing, and if the construction is pronounceable.

a Toscanini-ism
several Glenn Gould-isms
avoid
Vaughan Williams-isms

1.14. Group names. The name of a musical performance group should be given exactly as it appears according to a reliable source, such as a recording, letterhead, or official website. One of the biggest questions is whether an initial "the" is capitalized or lowercase. Capitalizing "the" if it is a documented part of the name is never wrong, and this is appropriate for some situations (concert programs, recordings). However, an essay with several group names with a mixture of both uppercase and lowercase articles—even if technically correct—would look inconsistent. So, it may be better to have "the" always lowercase for consistency. Note that a name that has no "the" may still need that article for the purpose of syntax, and if such an article is the first word in the sentence, it would be capitalized.

The Hanover Band
The Philadelphia Orchestra
The Who

Empire Brass
Kronos Quartet
Trans-Siberian Orchestra

The concert given by the Philadelphia Orchestra was . . .
The concert given by the Trans-Siberian Orchestra was . . .
The Empire Brass enjoys an international reputation . . .
    (this is a quote from their website)
not
The concert given by Trans-Siberian Orchestra was . . .

1.15. Groups with singular names. The name of a musical performance group is considered singular and therefore takes a singular verb. This is especially true if the name of the group contains a singular noun such as "band," "ensemble," "orchestra," "quartet," and so on. However, since these words are collective nouns—referring to a group of people—there are some circumstances in which the syntax requires a plural reference. If the reference is to the group as a whole, the singular is used; if the reference is to the group as individuals, the plural is used. If the plural construction seems awkward, reword the sentence using some sort of plural word.

The Philadelphia Orchestra is performing in its own concert hall.
but
The Philadelphia Orchestra are taking their seats.
or
The Philadelphia Orchestra members are taking their seats.

The Kronos Quartet is known for its interesting repertoire.
but
The Kronos Quartet are tuning their instruments.
or
The members of the Kronos Quartet are tuning their instruments.

1.16. Groups with plural names. Some names of musical performance groups are plural. Here, the singular verb may seem awkward, but rewording may avoid the problem. Notice the technique in the third sentence below of separating the plural name and the singular verb by an interposed singular noun.

The Swingle Singers are known for their vocal expertise.
but
The Swingle Singers is a unique vocal ensemble.
or
The Swingle Singers, a unique vocal ensemble, is . . .

There may be occasions in which a singular verb seems so awkward that it needs to be avoided. Use a plural verb or rewrite.

not
The Beatles is a major musical influence.
but
The Beatles are a major musical influence.
or
The Beatles, a musically influential group, is . . .
or
The members of the Beatles are musically influential.

Groups or collaborations that are known by two or more personal names also take a plural verb, unless the names are part of a company name.

Gilbert and Sullivan were . . .
Crosby, Stills, and Nash were . . .
Taylor and Boody are organbuilders who . . .
but
Taylor and Boody Organbuilders is a company that . . .

1.17. Hyphenation. The hyphenation of names is discussed in section 6.10.22.

2

Music Titles

2.1. Types of titles. The formal title of a musical composition may be a unique name, a generic name, or an incipit. In addition, a musical composition may have a subtitle given by the composer, or a nickname or popular name that may or may not have been given by the composer.

2.2. Unique titles. A unique title for a composition is one given by the composer and consists of one or more words that have not been used for other compositions. A unique title, especially of a stand-alone piece, is italicized, regardless of the length of the work.

Ionisation	*Rhapsody in Blue*
Die Kunst der Fuge	*Le sacre du printemps*
Messiah	*Short Ride in a Fast Machine*

2.3. Generic titles. A generic title for a composition consists of a word that is a genre (sonata, suite, symphony), a performance indication (adagio, allegro, maestoso), or a number-related instrumental combination (quartet, quintet, sextet) that has been used by a variety of composers or by the same composer more than once. Typically such a title has one or more identifiers that distinguish it in some way from other compositions with the same title (see sections 2.27–2.30). A generic title is in roman type and capitalized. A generic term used not as a title but as a generic term is lowercase.

Sonata no. 1
Suite no. 2
Symphony no. 3
but
A Scarlatti sonata differs from a Beethoven sonata.
A suite is a group of contrasting pieces.
There are two symphonies on tonight's program.

2.4. Generic title forms. For generic titles, a variety of forms may be acceptable if the composer's original indication is either unknown or is not specific enough for the purpose at hand (for example, if the original title page just says "Concerto"). For concert programs, the first version below is most appropriate. Opus numbers, catalog numbers, and year of composition may be added as needed (see sections 2.27–2.30); be careful to place such numbers so the resulting title is unambiguous. The use of ordinal designations (first, second, third, or the abbreviations 1st, 2nd, 3rd) may be used under some circumstances, but cardinal designations (no. 1, no. 2, no. 3) tend to offer a more consistent format, since there is debate among the style guides as to when one should use abbreviated versus written-out ordinals: some guides suggest written-out words only for numbers one through nine, some for one through ten, others for one through one hundred. Ordinals tend to be more useful not as title designations but when works are mentioned in passing, such as "There was quite a change in the composer's style between the first and second symphonies."

> Concerto no. 1 for Piano and Orchestra
> Piano Concerto no. 1
> First Piano Concerto
> *not*
> Concerto for Piano and Orchestra no. 1

> *preferably*: Symphony no. 41
> *if necessary*: 41st Symphony
> *try to avoid*: Forty-first Symphony

2.5. Generic terms italicized. If a generic term is incorporated in such a way as to form a unique title, it is italicized. However, following the guideline in section 2.3, individually numbered works of a uniquely titled set are not unique and would be in roman type. (The application of these two guidelines concurrently may require some flexibility.)

> Bach: *French Suites*   Copland: *A Dance Symphony*
> Brahms: *Tragic Overture*   Grofé: *Grand Canyon Suite*
> *but*
> Bach: French Suite no. 1, French Suite no. 2, . . .
> Stravinsky: Suite from *The Firebird*

2.6. Incipits. An incipit (Latin, "it begins") refers to the first few words of a vocal piece, or the first line of text on which a composition is based. An incipit is in roman type and quotation marks. Roman type is used even if the title is in a non-English language; italics and quotations marks are rarely used together.

"And the Glory of the Lord"
"Wachet auf, ruft uns die Stimme"

2.7. Non-English titles. Non-English titles may be treated in one of several ways. A work with a well-known non-English title retains that title and a translation may be added at its first occurrence. A work generally known by an English translation of its title retains the English title and mention may be made of the original. For a work that is known equally by either an original non-English title or an English translation, the writer may use one or the other, and the choice should be indicated (with preference given to the English version).

El amor brujo ("Love, the Magician")
La mer ("The Sea")

Academic Festival Overture (originally *Akademische Festouvertüre*)
The Four Seasons (originally *Le quattro stagioni*)

Le sacre du printemps (hereafter *The Rite of Spring*)
Das wohltemperirte Clavier (hereafter *The Well-Tempered Clavier*)

2.8. Capitalization. For non-English titles in running text, retain the original capitalization or lack thereof. In some contexts such as lists, tables, and concert programs, the title may be changed to headline-style capitalization. In certain situations, the use of headline style in running text for some well-known non-English titles (*Le Sacre du Printemps*, *Das Wohltemperirte Clavier*) may be considered an acceptable anglicization. However, some original titles are best left unchanged. When in doubt, consult an expert in the language. For English incipits, use sentence-style capitalization in running text and headline-style in lists. It should be mentioned that the capitalization of French titles shows considerable variation. With respect to the titles *La mer* and *Le sacre du printemps*, some people capitalize them just that way—first word only, as well as anything that would be capitalized in running text—while others recommend capitalizing "through the first noun" (*La Mer*, *Le Sacre du printemps*). In the absence of definitive rules, use sentence style unless there is a documented form by the composer or an expert advises you otherwise.

Running Text	Lists, Tables, and Programs
La mer	*La Mer*
Le sacre du printemps	*Le Sacre du Printemps*
Das wohltemperirte Clavier	*Das Wohltemperirte Clavier*
Prélude à "L'après-midi d'un faune"	(do not change)
"Ein' feste Burg ist unser Gott"	(do not change)
"I know that my Redeemer liveth"	"I Know That My Redeemer Liveth"

2.9. Subtitles. For a unique italicized title, a subtitle given by the composer is also italicized, set off from the main title by means of a colon and a space. For a generic English title in roman type, a subtitle is set in roman type and quotation marks, set off from the main title by the word "subtitled" to distinguish it from a popular name (see section 2.11). The inclusion of a non-English subtitle with or without a translation would be based on the intended readership of the essay or on musicological completeness.

Scott Joplin: *Solace: A Mexican Serenade*
Richard Strauss: *Don Quixote: Fantastische Variationen über ein Thema ritterlichen Charakters* ("Fantastic Variations on a Theme of Knightly Character")
Jean Sibelius: String Quartet in D minor, subtitled "Voces intimae"
Charles Ives: Piano Sonata no. 2, subtitled "Concord, Mass., 1840–1860"
Carl Nielsen: Symphony no. 4, subtitled "Det Uudslukkelige" ("The Inextinguishable")

2.10. Omitted subtitles. Some subtitles are not essential to identify a work and may be omitted. However, they may be mentioned for musicological completeness at their first occurrence or in a citation.

Don Quixote: Fantastische Variationen über ein Thema ritterlichen Charakters
reduced to
Don Quixote

The Rite of Spring: Scenes from Pagan Russia in Two Parts
reduced to
The Rite of Spring

2.11. Popular names. A popular name or nickname for a work is in roman type, quotation marks, and parentheses following the formal title of the work. Once the formal title has been given, the popular name may be used thereafter; however, a popular title may be inappropriate in some situations. The popular name should never be used without initially giving the formal title.

> F. J. Haydn: Symphony no. 94 in G major ("Surprise")
> (*optionally thereafter*, "Surprise" Symphony)

2.12. Popular names as titles. Some works have popular titles that are so entrenched in the musical literature that they are known more by that title than the composer's original appellation. These elevated popular names may be given in italics and used as an "official" title.

> J. S. Bach: *Goldberg Variations*
> instead of
> *Aria mit verschiedenen Veränderungen* ("Aria with Diverse Variations")

> Elgar: *Enigma Variations*
> instead of
> *Variations on an Original Theme*

> Grieg: *Holberg Suite*
> instead of
> *Fra Holbergs tid* ("From Holberg's Time")

> Johann Strauss Jr.: *The Blue Danube [Waltz]*
> instead of
> *An der schönen blauen Donau* ("On the Beautiful Blue Danube")

2.13. Exact titles. Apart from the situation mentioned in section 2.12, there may be the need for documenting an exact title for musicological correctness. Some titles have specific forms irrespective of popular usage; examples are given here.

    1. Claude Debussy's *Prélude à l'après-midi d'un faune* is a prelude based on a poem by Stéphane Mallarmé entitled "L'après-midi d'un faune." This means the musical work should most properly be referred to as *Prélude à "L'après-midi d'un faune"* with quotation marks.

    2. The various sections of G. F. Handel's *Messiah* use incipits as titles. Following this convention, "The Hallelujah Chorus" would be referred to as "Hallelujah."

3. The sonatas and partitas for solo violin by J. S. Bach were collectively called by him *Sei Solo*.

2.14. Colloquialisms and jargon. In formal writing, do not use colloquialisms or jargon from everyday speech as a substitute for a title.

not
Beethoven's Ninth (for Beethoven's Symphony no. 9)
the Brandenburgs (for the *Brandenburg Concertos*)
the "Jupiter" (for Mozart's Symphony no. 41)
Rach 3 (for Rachmaninoff's Piano Concerto no. 3)

2.15. Sections: Unique titles. For smaller sections of a uniquely titled larger work, use roman type and quotation marks. This applies even if the title of the smaller section is non-English. Use headline-style capitalization for English titles and original capitalization for non-English titles. This guideline, however, needs a degree of flexibility. For example, for a large-scale work whose component parts are also large-scale works, one could use italics for both. The type-format of other combination titles is based on whether the elements are unique titles, generic titles, or incipits. It may also be that the same piece could have a different format under different circumstances. For example, "Clair de lune" from Debussy's *Suite bergamasque* could be formatted as stated: roman type and quotation marks, especially if other sections of the suite are being discussed. Yet, the same piece could justifiably be given in italics because it is a unique title and is so well known that it could be discussed as a stand-alone work.

"Crucifixus" from *Mass in B minor*
"My Favorite Things" from *The Sound of Music*
"Won't Get Fooled Again" from *Who's Next*
but
Overture to *The Magic Flute*

Götterdämmerung from *Der Ring des Nibelungen*
  (two large-scale works)

"Komm, Jesu, komm zu deiner Kirche" from
  Cantata no. 61, "Nun komm, der Heiden Heiland"
  (two incipits)

"Clair de lune" from *Suite bergamasque*
   (when discussed as a section of the suite)
Clair de lune
   (when discussed as a stand-alone piece)

2.16. Sections: Generic titles. For smaller sections of a larger work in which both names are generic terms, use capitalized roman type for both. Multi-word titles are given in sentence-style capitalization.

Allegro from Sonata no. 1
Scherzo from Symphony no. 2
Allegro ma non troppo from Concerto no. 3

2.17. Sections: Three levels. For sections of works in which there are three levels—a piece is part of a larger work, and the latter is part of an even larger work or collection—the three levels are differentiated according to whether each is a unique title, a generic title, or an incipit, then the topmost level is additionally distinguished though the use of running text. As discussed above, sometimes a title may be formatted in more than one way; for example, "Les barricades mistérieuses" could be italicized if it is discussed as a stand-alone work because it is a unique title of a well-known piece.

Bach: Praeambulum from Partita no. 5, one of six partitas
   in *Clavier-Übung* I
F. Couperin: "Les barricades mistérieuses" from Ordre
   no. 6, from the second book of *Pièces de clavecin*
   ("Ordre no. 6" is anglicized; "*Sexième Ordre*" is the original)

2.18. Song titles. Song titles that are not part of a larger work are in roman type and quotation marks, capitalized headline-style. For non-English titles, use original capitalization and no italics.

"White Christmas"   "Sur le Pont d'Avignon"
"Knowing Me, Knowing You"

2.19. Shortened titles. Long titles, once they are mentioned in full, may be shortened in running text for simplicity. Take care to devise a short title that is unambiguous. One solution is to extract one or two words from the title. Another solution is to use an ellipsis (. . .), although such constructions sometimes interfere with readability.

Hindemith: *Symphonic Metamorphosis on Themes by*
    Carl Maria von Weber
use *Symphonic Metamorphosis*

John Adams: *I Was Looking at the Ceiling and Then I Saw the Sky*
use *Ceiling/Sky* (this was used by the composer himself)

Erik Satie: *Three Pieces in the Form of a Pear*
use *Three . . . Pear*, or *Three Pieces* (if unambiguous)

Alan Hohvaness: *And God Created Great Whales*
use *Great Whales*

Harry Partch: *And on the Seventh Day Petals Fell in Petaluma*
use *Petaluma*

2.20. Commercial titles. In formal writing, do not use a commercially related name as an identifier of a work. The exception is if one needs to specifically mention the title of a recording with such a reference.

not
"The Lone Ranger" Overture (for Overture to *Guillaume Tell*)
Mouret's *Masterpiece Theatre* theme (for Rondeau from
    Sinfonies de Fanfares)
Richard Strauss's 2001 Tone Poem (for *Also sprach Zarathustra*)

2.21. Liturgical titles. Titles of Latin liturgical works are set in roman type and capitalized.

Agnus Dei	Gloria	Mass
Benedictus	Kyrie	Requiem
Credo	Magnificat	Sanctus

but
Leonard Bernstein's *Mass*
(this is a theater piece, not a setting of the liturgy)

2.22. Hymn tunes. For titles of hymn tunes, set them apart from the surrounding text by the use of small capitals after the initial capital letter.

the hymn tune SINE NOMINE by Ralph Vaughan Williams

2.23. Titles as singular. Titles are singular nouns and therefore take a singular verb; this includes musical compositions with plural titles. If the sentence sounds awkward when spoken aloud, consider rewording it. (This is less troublesome for non-English plural titles in an English context.) Related to this is the fact that a title is not interchangeable with the subject to which it refers.

Chichester Psalms is published by . . .
not
Chichester Psalms are published by . . .

alternatively
The composition *Chichester Psalms* is . . .
or
Chichester Psalms, composed in 1965, is . . .

Bach wrote a work now called the *Italian Concerto*.
Bach understood well the elements of the Italian concerto.
not
The *Italian Concerto*—a genre Bach knew well—is . . .

Alice Goodman wrote the libretto for *Nixon in China*.
Alice Goodman wrote a libretto about Nixon in China.

2.24. Articles as part of title. The definite article "the" and the indefinite articles "a" and "an" are sometimes part of the title of a musical work. Given the syntax, occasionally there is a problem in running text with these articles. The first thing to ascertain is whether an article is part of the official title.

Fontane di Roma, Fountains of Rome
Musikalisches Opfer, Musical Offering
Tragische Ouvertüre, Tragic Overture

A Midsummer Night's Dream
A Sea Symphony
Ein deutsches Requiem, A German Requiem

Die Kunst der Fuge, The Art of Fugue
Le quattro stagioni, The Four Seasons
L'histoire du soldat, The Soldier's Tale

but
"Der Tod und das Mädchen," "Death and the Maiden"
La Cenerentola, Cinderella
Le roi David, King David

2.25. Article retained or omitted. For English titles and translations of non-English titles, the first choice is not to omit the article and rewrite the sentence to accommodate the original article. If this cannot be done, the article may be omitted if the syntax needs to be accommodated. The most common circumstance in which articles are omitted is when the possessive form of the composer's name precedes the title. Non-English titles retain the article.

We will be performing *A German Requiem, The Four Seasons,* and *L'histoire du soldat.*
or
We will be performing Brahms's *German Requiem,* Vivaldi's *Four Seasons,* and Stravinsky's *L'histoire du soldat.*

Bach composed the *Italian Concerto* for a two-manual harpsichord.
not
Bach composed *Italian Concerto* . . .
not
Bach composed *The Italian Concerto* . . .

Bach composed *The Art of Fugue* ca. 1745–50.
not
Bach composed the *Art of Fugue* . . .

2.26. Other first words. Titles that begin with words that are not nouns or articles must be left "as is" regardless of the resulting syntax. Rewriting such sentences may improve readability, although this is less critical for non-English titles.

For *Für Elise,* . . .
For *Pour le piano,* . . .
The ensemble performed "Crucifixus" and "Et resurrexit."

instead of
In "In dulci jubilo," BWV 608, Bach uses a canon.
rather
In the piece "In dulci jubilo," BWV 608, Bach uses a canon.

instead of
We performed *Alleluia and Fugue* and *And God Created
Great Whales* by Alan Hovhaness.

rather
We performed two works by Alan Hovhaness: *And God
Created Great Whales* (1970) as well as *Alleluia
and Fugue* (1941).

2.27. Opus and number. The use of the designations "opus" and "number" in running text have the following form: abbreviated, roman type, lowercase, followed by a period, space, and an arabic numeral, with commas before and after. Commas are not used when "no." is a genre designation ("Symphony no. 5"). While the majority of the style guides that were reviewed recommend lowercase for the abbreviations "op." and "no.", this practice varies; capitalized abbreviations are often found. Generally speaking, however, capitals should be used frugally. Capitalized designations are probably more suitable for pieces listed in a concert program. Whether one uses lowercase or uppercase in running text, be consistent. Providing there is no chance of ambiguity, opus designations may be omitted subsequent to their first occurrence.

Running text
Brahms's *Academic Festival Overture*, op. 80, was written in 1880.
Grieg's piece *The Last Spring*, op. 34, no. 2, exists in an
    orchestral version and a piano version.
Beethoven's Symphony no. 5, op. 67, is in four movements.

Program format
Johannes Brahms: *Academic Festival Overture*, Op. 80
Edvard Grieg: *The Last Spring*, Op. 34, No. 2
Ludwig van Beethoven: Symphony No. 5, Op. 67

2.28. Catalog designation. The use of a catalog designation has the following form: capitalized, period, space, arabic numeral, with commas before and after. The exceptions are BWV, BuxWV, HWV, and so on, which have no periods. The Hoboken designation for the works of F. J. Haydn has a roman numeral and colon added; there is a space after "Hob." or "H." (although some references prefer no space) and no space following the roman numeral. Some references prefer to use smaller type for a catalog reference (BWV 245 as opposed to BWV 245).

This is most useful in an index to differentiate a catalog number from a page number.

Bach's Brandenburg Concerto no. 3, BWV 1048, is . . .
Mozart's Symphony no. 35 in D major, K. 385, is . . .
Haydn's Symphony no. 100, Hob. I:100, is . . . (*or* H. I:100)
in an index: *St. John Passion*, BWV 245, 246, 249
not
BWV1048 (closed)
K385 (no period, closed)

2.29. Opus and catalog designation usage. When an opus or catalog designation is used as the only identifier to a generic title, or when an opus number is used alone as a substitute title, there are no commas. In such a circumstance, the word "opus" may even be spelled out. (The word "opus" should definitely be spelled out if it starts a sentence.) The use of "no." or "nos." in some circumstances is acceptable and could remain abbreviated to avoid ambiguity. An opus or catalog designation by itself should only be used after the full title of the work is given at its first mention in the text. The use of the composer's name with just a catalog designation may be considered redundant, providing the composer's name has already been mentioned. The only reason to use the composer's name with a catalog designation would be to avoid ambiguity; for example, if one happened to be discussing both Mozart and D. Scarlatti, one would need to make the distinction between "K" for Köchel and "K" for Kirkpatrick. (Possibilities are "Kk" or "Kp" for Kirkpatrick, although one needs to be careful about inventing identifiers that may not be widely accepted.)

Beethoven's Symphony op. 67 was on the program.
Beethoven's op. 67 was . . . (*or* Beethoven's opus 67)

Bach's Cantata BWV 80 was . . .
Bach's Cantata no. 80 was . . .

Of Bach's keyboard partitas, nos. 1, 4, and 5 are in major keys.

The ensemble will perform BWV 80 . . .
    (*not* Bach's BWV 80)

The orchestra will perform K. 385 . . .
    (*not* Mozart's K. 385)

2.30. Year. If a work has no opus or catalog number, the year of its completion may be included. The year is placed in parentheses after the title. If there is a particular version of a work, indicate this inside the parentheses with the year. If there are several additional dates that could be included—first performance, revisions—incorporate these into the text rather than parenthetically after the title. For works that have either an opus number or a catalog number or both, including a year may be done if there is a reason; for example, for an essay on the chronology of a composer's works. Sometimes incorporating the year in the running text instead of parenthetically may help readability. For situations in which a parenthetical statement already exists—such as a translation—incorporate the year into the existing parentheses or set it into the running text.

> Hindemith's Concerto for Piano and Orchestra (1945) is . . .
> Stravinsky's Suite from *The Firebird* (1919 version) is . . .
> Completed in the year 1823, Schubert's *Die schöne Müllerin*,
>   op. 25, D. 795, is . . .
> Ravel's *Ma mère l'oye* ("Mother Goose Suite," 1908–10) is . . .
> Originally composed in 1908–10 for piano four-hands,
>   Ravel's *Ma mère l'oye* ("Mother Goose Suite") is . . .

2.31. Movements. Reference to a particular movement in a multi-movement work may be done by means of ordinal numbers, the tempo indication, or the genre. Either the preposition "of" or "from" may be used, depending on the context.

> the third movement of the Symphony no. 6
>   (*not* movement no. 3, movement 3, movement three)
> the Allegro from Symphony no. 6
> the Scherzo from the Symphony no. 6

Some writers favor a shorthand approach for designating movements. This is most appropriate for tables in which space is limited. Its use in running text is debatable, the biggest objection being that such notation does not "read" well. Avoid arabic superscripts, as these may be mistaken for footnotes or endnotes. Lowercase letters should not be used; these are reserved for documenting alternate versions of the same work (for example, BWV 545, BWV 545a, and BWV 545b). To this author, the first or second example given here looks the best in running text in terms of being unambiguous and uncluttered.

op. 67iii	BWV 525iii
op. 67.iii	BWV 525.iii
op. 67/iii	BWV 525/iii
op. 67^{III}	BWV 525^{III}
op. 67/3	BWV 525/3

2.32. Composer identification. When a composer's name is given along with the title of a piece in running text, this may be as the possessive form of the name preceding the title, or with the word "by" and the name following the title. The use of the composer's name followed by a semicolon should be reserved for lists, as is done with many of the examples in this chapter. Avoid the use of the word "of" with a composer's name as a substitute for "by." Avoid the insertion of a composer's name after "the" when referring to a work in formal writing. While it may be used in some contexts as a convenient indicator of previously mentioned works when being compared or contrasted with other works, try rewording the sentence.

> as seen in Beethoven's Symphony no. 5
> *or*
> as seen in the Symphony no. 5 by Beethoven

> *not*
> in Beethoven: Symphony no. 5
> in the Beethoven Symphony no. 5
> in the Symphony no. 5 of Beethoven

> *not*
> Which is your favorite violin concerto:
>   the Beethoven or the Mendelssohn?
> *rather*
> Which is your favorite violin concerto:
>   Beethoven's or Mendelssohn's?

2.33. Possessive of title. There may be some circumstances in which the description of an attribute of a work may involve using the possessive form of a title, with an apostrophe and an *s* ('s). Whether the title is in roman or italic type, put apostrophe-S in roman type. However, this construction should be limited to those select cases in which the term is easily formed and readable; otherwise, reword the sentence using "of." Titles with quotation marks should not be converted to a possessive form with apostrophe-S but should be phrased using the word "of."

the Sonata's dynamics
Messiah's performance history

not
the Sonata no. 5's dynamics
but
the dynamics in the Sonata no. 5

not
"White Christmas's" popularity *or* "White Christmas"'s popularity
but
the popularity of "White Christmas"

not
the *Symphonic Metamorphosis*'s harmonic progressions
but
the harmonic progressions in the *Symphonic Metamorphosis*

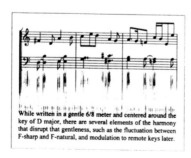

While written in a gentle 6/8 meter and centered around the
key of D major, there are several elements of the harmony
that disrupt that gentleness, such as the fluctuation between
F-sharp and F-natural, and modulation to remote keys later.

3

Notes and Pitches

3.1. Note names. Note names are set in roman capital letters for the following categories:

1. Generic note references ("the orchestra tunes to an A")
2. Note names (middle C)
3. Keys (D major, G minor)
4. Chords with a note name (F-major triad)
5. Scales with a note name (A-major scale)
6. Clefs with a note name (G clef, C clef)
7. Instruments (D trumpet, F tuba)
8. Elements of an instrument ("the C keys on a piano," "the E string of a violin")

3.2. Accidentals: Word or sign. An accidental is represented in running text by appending a note name with one of the following: (1) the word written out in lowercase roman type, hyphenated to the note name; or (2) the corresponding sign immediately following the note name without a space. Depending on the context, there may need to be an additional hyphen for the terms "double sharp" and "double flat" for clarity.

C-sharp	*or*	C♯
B-flat		B♭
D-natural		D♮
C-double-sharp		C𝄪
B-double-flat		B♭♭

3.3. Accidentals: Sign usage. For accidentals, both signs and written-out words are used and accepted equally. Whichever is used in running text, be consistent. Signs should only be used in conjunction with a note name, never by themselves in place of the words "sharp" and "flat." If there are a great many notes, keys, chords, or scales mentioned in an essay, signs may assist readability. Signs are also more compact for tables.

the key of A-flat major
or
the key of A♭ major

The piece has a key signature with one flat.
not
The piece has a key signature with one ♭.

In meantone temperament, the usual accidentals are C♯, E♭, F♯, G♯, and B♭, not D♭, D♯, G♭, A♭, and A♯.

3.4. Accidentals: Alternate signs. In formal writing, use the actual signs for sharp, flat, natural, and double sharp rather than substitute characters. It must be admitted that in some circumstances, the pound sign may be an acceptable substitute for the sharp sign if only the sharp sign is being used to a limited degree.

C♯ *not* C# (pound or number sign)
B♭ *not* Bb (lowercase *b*)
D𝄪 *not* Dx (lowercase *x*), *not* D× (multiplication sign)

3.5. Accidentals: Sign placement. Align sharp and flat signs on the baseline rather than as subscripts or superscripts. It should be noted that some typefaces have the flat sign slightly raised (E♭ as opposed to E♭) and this may be considered acceptable.

C♯, *not* C♯, C♯, C♯, *or* C♯
E♭, *not* E♭, E♭, E♭, *or* E♭

3.6. Note plurals. Plurals for notes are formed by adding an *s* without an apostrophe. Consider rewriting the sentence to avoid plurals.

Cs, F-sharps, F♯s, B-flats, B♭s
not
C's, F-sharp's, F♯'s, B-flat's, B♭'s

not

There are too many B♭s.

but

There are too many B♭ notes.

3.7. German notation. German designation of notes includes B for B-flat, H for B-natural, Es for E-flat, and As for A-flat. Be careful about constructing sentences that may be misread; for example, "Es" may mean plural *E* or German E-flat, and "As" may mean plural *A*, the German A-flat, or capitalized "as." Reword the sentence for clarity. Do not use the German notes unless dictated by the context, such as discussing the B–A–C–H motif or quoting a treatise. If the German notation is necessary, be sure to alert the reader as to its meaning.

There are many works that use the B–A–C–H motif, which is the German notation for the note sequence B♭–A–C–B♮.

The illustration of the keyboard shows it extending down to B-natural, labeled "H" in the German original.

not

The key of B has two flats. (German notation here is unacceptable.)

avoid

As far as As and Es . . .

3.8. Major and minor. Use lowercase roman type when using the terms "major" and "minor" in conjunction with note names for keys, scales, and chords. Each term is not hyphenated to the note name with which it is associated if the term is being used by itself, but would be hyphenated when it is being used as a modifier or compound adjective.

This piece is in the key of D minor.

but

Notice the change of mood in the piece at the D-minor chord.

The key signature of E-flat major has three flats.

but

The E-flat-major sonata is one of my favorites.

Of the preludes, the D-major is the most challenging.

3.9. Major and minor: Inclusion. Do not omit the term "major" when discussing a major key.

not
This piece is in the key of D.
Bach's Fugue in E-flat is in three parts.

3.10. Major and minor: Capitalization. Do not capitalize the words "major" and "minor" in running text; reserve capitalization for proper names and proper adjectives, and otherwise use it frugally. Avoid the convention of having the word "major" always capitalized and the word "minor" always lowercase. Also avoid the use of lowercase note names with the word "minor."

Symphony no. 3 in E-flat major
Symphony no. 5 in C minor
not
Symphony no. 5 in c minor

3.11. Major and minor: Abbreviated forms. Some abbreviated forms for the designations "major" and "minor" are shown here. While one should avoid abbreviations in running text, they may be useful when it is necessary to save space in a table. An exception for running text is if there is an extended discussion of keys. In the event any of these alternates are employed, alert the reader to their use. Avoid mixing formats, such as "C maj." with "C minor", or "C major" with "Cm."

Major	Minor	
C	c	(most common, recommended)
C maj.	C min.	
CM	Cm	(least common)

The pianist performed the preludes in C major and C minor.
not
The pianist performed the preludes in C and c.

but
Bach's *French Suites* are in the keys of d, c, b, E♭, G, and E;
    the *English Suites* are in the keys of A, a, g, F, e, and d;
    and the Partitas are in the keys of B♭, c, a, D, G, and e.

3.12. Major and minor: Starting a sentence. Sentences that begin with "A major" or "A minor" may cause the reader to misread them since such terms may refer to (1) a specific key, scale, or chord based on the note A; (2) any key, scale, or chord based on a major or minor scale; or (3) the meaning "great or lesser in importance" (such as, "a major accomplishment" and "a minor inconvenience"). Instead, reword the sentence.

not
A minor is the key of piano concertos by Schumann and Grieg.
but
The key of A minor was used by Schumann and Grieg for their piano concertos.

not
A minor key sometimes conveys sadness.
but
Sadness is sometimes conveyed through the use of a minor key.

not
A major symphony by Smith will be premièred.
but
The orchestra will première a major symphony by Smith.

3.13. Octave designation. When identifying specific pitches in running text, some sort of notation system is required to differentiate higher or lower pitches with the same note name. Such a system is referred to as an *octave designation* or a *staff-independent notation*. Table 3.1 lists a variety of these systems.

The systems are separated into three categories, in which middle C is designated as either a lowercase letter with a single-character superscript (c′ or c^1), a lowercase letter without a qualifying character (c), or an uppercase letter with a unique numbering sequence. The first category is based on the system used by Hermann von Helmholtz in *Die Lehre von den Tonempfindugen* ("On the Sensations of Tone," 1863). As shown by the number of references listed in table 3.1, this is the most widely represented category. Apparently it is based on designating the lowest note on an organ keyboard with the uppercase letter "C." System 5 with its horizontal lines is rarely seen; typically this category is represented by superscript primes or superscript numerals. Note the consistent plan in all systems in this category for the

Table 3.1. Octave Designation (Staff-Independent Notation)

Middle C = c' or c¹			↓			
1. Helmholtz[a]	C,	C	c	c'	c"	c'''	c''''
2. HDM #1[b]	C_1	C	c	c'	c"	c'''	c''''
3. GMO,[a] JSCM,[c]	C'	C	c	c'	c"	c'''	c''''
4. Hubbard[d]	CC	C	c	c'	c"	c'''	c''''
5. Helmholtz variant[e]	CC	C	c	$\bar{c}$	$\bar{\bar{c}}$	$\bar{\bar{\bar{c}}}$	$\bar{\bar{\bar{\bar{c}}}}$
6. Brauchli,[f] Irvine #3[g]	C_1	C	c	c^1	c^2	c^3	c^4
7. Holoman,[h] Kottick[i]	CC	C	c	c^1	c^2	c^3	c^4
8. OHS[j]	CCC	CC	c^0	c^1	c^2	c^3	c^4
9. Audsley[k]	CCC	CC	C	c^1	c^2	c^3	c^4

Middle C = c						
10. HDM #2,[b] Irvine #2[g]	CCC	CC	C	c	c'	c"	c'''
11. HDM #3,[b] Notes[l]	C_2	C_1	C	c	c^1	c^2	c^3

Miscellaneous Numberings						
12. Young,[e] Irvine #1[g]	C_3	C_2	C_1	C	C^1	C^2	C^3
13. Scientific (ASA)[m]	C1	C2	C3	C4	C5	C6	C7
14. $C_0 = 1$ Hz[e]	C_5	C_6	C_7	C_8	C_9	C_{10}	C_{11}
15. Organ keyboard	—	C1	C13	C25	C37	C49	C61
16. Piano keyboard	C4	C16	C28	C40	C52	C64	C76

The arrow designates middle C.

a. "Pitch Nomenclature," *Grove Music Online*, Laura Macy, ed., http://www.grovemusic.com.

b. "Pitch Names," *The New Harvard Dictionary of Music*, Don Michael Randel, ed. (Cambridge, Mass.: The Belknap Press of Harvard University Press, 1986).

c. "Punctuation, Text Style, and Symbols," *Style Sheet*, Journal of Seventeenth-Century Music, 2006. http://www.sscm-jscm.org.

d. Frank Hubbard, *Three Centuries of Harpsichord Making* (Cambridge, Mass.: Harvard University Press, 1967), 5.

e. Robert W. Young, "A Staveless Notation," *Journal of Musicology* 1, no. 2 (September 1939), 8.

f. Bernard Brauchli, *The Clavichord* (Cambridge: Cambridge University Press, 1998), 4.

Table 3.1 *continued*

---

g. Demar Irvine, *Irvine's Writing about Music*, 3rd ed., rev. and enlarged by Mark A. Radice (Portland, Ore.: Amadeus Press, 1999), 201–3.

h. D. Kern Holoman, *Writing about Music: A Style Sheet from the Editors of 19th-Century Music* (Berkeley: University of California Press, 1988), 7.

i. Edward L. Kottick, *The Harpsichord Owner's Guide* (Chapel Hill: University of North Carolina Press, 1987), x.

j. Organ Historical Society Press, *Style Sheet* (Richmond, Va.: OHS Press, n.d.), 5.

k. George Ashdown Audsley, *The Art of Organ-Building*, 2 vols. (Reprint, New York: Dover, 1965): II:23–24.

l. "Keys, Letters, Pitches, Syllables, and Symbols," James P. Cassaro et al., *Notes Style Sheet*, Music Library Association, 2006. http://www.areditions.com/mla/notes/stylesheet.html.

m. The Acoustical Society of America; see John Backus, *The Acoustical Foundations of Music*, 2nd ed. (New York: W. W. Norton, 1977), 154.

octaves above middle C, in which the numeral or the number of primes increases to two, three, four, and so on. Note also that the majority of the systems use a lowercase letter for the octave below middle C and an uppercase letter for two octaves below middle C. The only widely divergent notation is that for the C three octaves below middle C. Systems 8 and 9 are rather distinctive in their notation below middle C.

The second category is apparently not based on the organ keyboard but on the gamut, as found in Robert Smith's *Harmonics* (1748). Here, middle C is designated with an unqualified lowercase letter. Then, all octaves above middle C are designated with lowercase letters plus superscripts, while all octaves below middle C are designated with uppercase letters. Notice that there is a mismatch between the first and second categories with respect to what c' or c^1 represents.

The third category represents several systems whose underlying principle is to use numbers to qualify an uppercase letter based on different frames of reference. System 12 designates middle C with an uppercase letter, then designates upper octaves with superscripts and lower octaves with subscripts. System 13 is based on the keyboard of the modern piano with 88 keys: the lowest C on the keyboard is designated C1, and each succeeding higher octave has its number increased by one. This is particularly favored in scientific circles. (With systems 13 through 16, the numbers used have been variously notated as baseline numbers, superscripts, or subscripts.) System 14 is based on using the designation C_0 for a frequency of 1 hertz (Hz). Then, C_1 is 2 Hz, C_3

is 4 Hz, and so on, with middle C being C_8. System 15 is based on a convention used by organbuilders of simply numbering the keys on the keyboard consecutively from two octaves below middle C. This system assumes a completely chromatic keyboard (no short octaves). System 16 uses the same approach but in terms of the 88-key piano keyboard.

Each system has advantages and disadvantages, and depending on the focus of one's writing, one system may prove useful over another, and a specialized system may prove more appropriate than a consensus system under some circumstances. Of those in the third category, systems 13, 15, and 16 are commonly used in their respective fields. For a consensus system, the first category seems a better choice by virtue of the greater number of references that designate c′ or c¹ as middle C. A recommendation would be either system 4 or system 7, which are identical except for the difference of primes vs. numerical superscripts. The advantage to these two systems has to do with the designation for three octaves below middle C. The designation C′ means one octave *below* C, while the designation c′ means one octave *above* c; in other words, the prime sign is signifying two different things. On the other hand, the use of CC as one octave below C is a unique designation and carries with it a certain degree of "visual weight" commensurate with that lower range. So, a recommended system for octave designation is as follows (with the arrow indicating middle C):

$$\downarrow$$

$$CC \quad C \quad c \quad c' \quad c'' \quad c''' \quad c''''$$
$$or$$
$$CC \quad C \quad c \quad c^1 \quad c^2 \quad c^3 \quad c^4$$

Notice the use of italics. This helps to differentiate the specific pitch *C* from the generic note name C, the numerical superscripts from citation numbering, and the pitches *a* and *A* from the indefinite article "a" or "A." Whatever system is chosen, inform the reader about the designations for each C note, and what designation represents middle C.

3.14. Conversions. An alternate purpose for listing all the systems in table 3.1 is to allow conversion among them. If material is quoted from a source that uses a system different from the one you are using, note this in the text.

> The range given by Smith is from G3 to D5 (this is equivalent
> to our use of *g* to d^2).

3.15. Non-C pitches. Specific pitches between the C landmarks use the designation of the octave they are in; for example, the B below middle C is b, the A above middle C is a' or a^1. Accidentals below C (with double capital letters) are given just one sign. Accidental signs for pitches above middle C are placed between the note name and the superscript.

$GG\#$ not $G\#G\#$	$g\#^1$ not $g^1\#$
$BB\flat$ not $B\flat B\flat$	$b\flat^2$ not $b^2\flat$

3.16. Awkward juxtapositions. Avoid sentence constructions that place quotation marks near primes and citation numbers near numerical superscripts, especially mid-sentence. Do not start a sentence with a lowercase pitch designation.

not
Smith wrote, "The highest note is c''' " in her analysis.
The claim that the highest note is $c^{3\,2}$ appears to be correct.

not
c^1 represents middle C in this essay.
but
In this essay, c^1 represents middle C.

3.17. C names. Unique names for the different C notes may be useful in some circumstances to offer the writer alternate methods of expressing notes in running text and to allow the reader to have a pronunciation for the notation used. Possible names are given in table 3.2.

Table 3.2. Names for C Notes

CC	contra C		
C	great C		
c	tenor C, small C		
c^1, c'	middle C	one-line C	C prime
c^2, c''	treble C	two-line C	C double-prime
c^3, c'''		three-line C	C triple-prime
c^4, c''''		four-line C	C quadruple-prime

Notice that ambiguous names such as "low C" or "high C" are avoided, and the writer should probably avoid them also. While a pronounceable name has advantages, an octave designation system from table 3.1 offers clarity. The writer should also be aware that some readers may have their own pronunciations that would be inappropriate in formal writing, such as "C two" for c^2 and "C three" for c^3.

3.18. Non-C names. Note names between the C notes may be indicated by the octave designation name, or in relation to the nearest C. Again, use these names in running text only when they promote clarity, since some names may be too complex (such as "F-sharp double-prime").

for *G*:	great G *or* the G above great C *or* the G below tenor C
for *f*:	tenor F *or* the F above tenor C *or* the F below middle C
for a^1:	one-line A *or* A prime *or* the A above middle C
	(be careful "A prime" is not confused with the
	phrase "A prime example of . . .")
for e^2:	two-line E *or* E double-prime

3.19. Enharmonics. The note C♭ that is enharmonically the same as the B below middle C is considered part of the middle (one-line) octave and so is notated cb^1. Similarly, the note B♯ that is enharmonically the same as middle C is considered part of the tenor octave and so is notated *b♯*. Other notes are notated similarly.

3.20. Note series. A series of consecutive notes representing a melodic motif or phrase are connected with en dashes and no spaces. Use uppercase roman letters for generic note references and italics for exact pitches.

The sequence D–C♯–C♮–B–B♭–A is known as the chromatic fourth.
The violins played the note sequence d^2–$c\sharp^2$–$c\natural^2$–b^1–bb^1–a^1.

3.21. Intervals. For representing an interval—two notes or pitches sounding simultaneously—a hyphen or an en dash may be used between the note names.

the interval C-G   *or*   the interval C–G

Usually, an en dash stands for the word "to" and is used for a range of page numbers, times, or dates. For example, "pp. 34–41" means "pages

34 to 41" and "1685–1750" means "[the years] 1685 to 1750." In this respect, a hyphen may be more appropriate for indicating intervals, since one of its functions is to tie words together.

3.22. Tunings. For references to the tuning of stringed instruments, use exact pitches with en dashes.

A common tuning for the modern guitar is $E–A–d–g–b–e^1$.

3.23. Grouped notes. Three note names representing a triad may be grouped with plus signs. This is a visual clue that the notes are sounded simultaneously instead of sequentially, but the use of hyphens in place of plus signs in a properly worded sentence would also be appropriate.

A C-major triad in root position is C+E+G.
The first inversion of a C-major triad is E-G-C.

3.24. Keyboard compass. The following are representative descriptions of keyboard compasses using octave designations.

$CCC–c^5$ (97 notes), Bösendorfer model 290 piano
$AAA–c^5$ (88 notes), modern piano keyboard
$FF–f^3$ (61 notes), five-octave harpsichord keyboard
$C–c^4$ (61 notes), five-octave organ manual keyboard
$CD–c^3$ (no $C\sharp$; 48 notes)
$FG–g^2a^2$ (no $F\sharp$ or $g\sharp^2$; 39 notes)
$C/E–c^3$ or $CDEFGA–c^3$ (short octave; apparent range E to c^3;
$\quad$ E key sounds C; $F\sharp$ key sounds D; $G\sharp$ key sounds E;
$\quad$ F and G keys sound their usual notes; then chromatic
$\quad$ from A to c^3; 45 notes)
$GG/BB–d^3$ or $GGAABBCDE–d^3$ (apparent range BB to d^3;
$\quad$ BB key sounds GG, $C\sharp$ key sounds AA, $D\sharp$ key sounds BB;
$\quad$ C and D keys sound their usual notes; then chromatic
$\quad$ from E to d^3; 52 notes)

3.25. Organ keyboards. For organs, the compass designation for the pedal keyboard is no different than that used for the manual keyboard. The fact that an organ has differently pitched pipes is irrelevant to the keyboard compass. So, a pedal keyboard that starts at a C and extends for 30 notes would be designated $C–f^1$ (in the recommended system mentioned above). Some writers use a combination notation for both manual and pedal keyboards together; if the manual compass is C–g^3 and the pedal compass is C–f^1, this is sometimes given as C–f^1–g^3.

3.26. Pitch range. When discussing a range of pitches, use an en dash to connect the two pitch extremes. If the pitch range is preceded by the word "from," use the word "to" in place of the en dash. Likewise, if the pitch range is preceded by the word "between," use the word "and" in place of the en dash.

> Handel's harpsichord music lies within a GG–d^3 range.
> *but*
> The range of this song is from g to b^2.
> Keep the vocal range of the hymn between bb and d^2.

3.27. Pitch reference. The terms *pitch reference* or *pitch level* refer to the standardized association of a particular frequency with a note name. When referring to a pitch reference, using the specific note name avoids ambiguity; this is usually the A above middle C (a^1) or the C an octave above middle C (c^2). An acceptable shorthand method—providing the reader is informed—involves the use of a capital roman letter and the frequency.

> a^1 = 415 Hz   *or*   A415
> a^1 = 440 Hz   A440
> c^2 = 493 Hz   C493
> c^2 = 523 Hz   C523

3.28. Transposing instruments. For some instruments, their sounding pitches differ from the notation of those pitches; for example, guitar music is notated an octave higher than the sounding pitches. With respect to using an octave designation system, a discussion of the music for such transposing instruments should be in terms of the notated pitch, while a discussion of the nature of the sounding pitches should be in terms of the actual pitch. In the interest of clarity, it may be best for some situations to mention both the sounding and notated pitches.

> The guitar arrangement of the piece has no note higher than e^2.

> The top string of the guitar—notated e^2 but sounding e^1—
>   has a frequency of about 330 Hz.

4

Letters and Numbers

Opus numbers and catalog numbers are discussed in chapter 2. Notes and pitches are discussed in chapter 3.

4.1. Form. The form of a piece may be indicated by the use of a series of uppercase roman letters (A, B, C, and so on) without spaces or en dashes. Each different letter represents a well-defined section. The prime sign designates a section musically similar to a previous one but varied in some way. Numerical subscripts are sometimes used. For solo concertos, R and S may be used to represent the ritornello and solo sections respectively. When referring to individual sections by letter, be aware that it may be necessary to use the word "section" or "part" ("the motif in section A") and to phrase the sentence in such a way that the section letter is not misread as a note name.

binary form: AA′
ternary form: ABA, ABA′
rondo: ABACA, ABACBA, ABACABA, etc.
solo concerto: $R_1S_1R_2S_2 \ldots$

4.2. Harmony. Roman numerals indicate harmony according to the degrees of the scale; connecting such numerals with en dashes indicates harmonic progressions. Uppercase roman numerals refer to major chords, lowercase to minor chords. For harmonic progressions in specific tonalities, uppercase and lowercase note names are used.

The harmonic progressions V–I and V–vi are considered strong, while IV–I is considered weak.

I–V–vi–iii–IV–I–IV–V *or* D–A–b–f♯–G–D–G–A

4.3. Chords. A generic reference to the notes of single chords is notated with roman uppercase letters; a reference to specific pitches is notated with italics according to a selected octave designation system.

In either case, the letters are connected with hyphens. Under some circumstances, it may be better to write out the name of the chord, if such a name exists. Modifications to chords—inversions, seventh chords, etc.—may be notated using roman numerals with arabic superscripts and subscripts. More complex figured-bass notation may need to be integrated within the context of a musical example.

> the chord C-E♭-F♯-A (the hyphen signifies simultaneity)
> the chord B-D-G, *or* the chord *b-d^l-g^l*

> diminished seventh chord
> six-four chord, *or* 6-4 chord (*not* 6/4 chord *or* 64 chord)

> the progression I–vi–ii–V–1
> the progression I–I^6–IV–I–V$^6_5$ –I–V
> (the en dash signifies a sequence)

> V$^6_5$ chord, *or* six-five chord on V, *or* 6-5 chord on V,
> *or*, dominant seventh chord in second inversion

4.4. Measure numbers. When indicating specific musical passages to the reader by means of measure numbers, the following conventions are recommended. If the measures are numbered in the edition at hand, use those. If measure numbers are not provided, number them yourself. The use of the abbreviations "m." and "mm." for "measure" and "measures" in running text is acceptable if they are followed by a number. Use an en dash to indicate a range of measure numbers, but use the word "to" if the sentence contains the word "from" and use the word "and" if the sentence contains the word "between."

> the chord in m. 21 is . . .
> the chord progression in mm. 21–25 is . . .

> *but*
> the phrase extending from m. 25 to m. 30
> the composer's markings between m. 32 and m. 36

> *not*
> the phrase extending from mm. 25–30
> the composer's markings between mm. 32–36

4.5. Measure subdivisions. Some writers use superscripts to designate beats in a measure; for example, the first and second beats in measure 36 would be written "m. 36^{1-2}." One may even use this method for a range; for example, from the third beat in measure 20 to the first beat in measure 25 would be written "mm. 20^3–25^1." This is acceptable providing the superscripts are not misinterpreted as footnotes or endnotes; however, many readers may find it difficult to see the superscripts as anything but citations. A shorthand method may be most useful as a space-saving device in tables, in captions for musical examples, or when there is an extensive discussion of measure subdivisions. The advantage of any such shorthand notation needs to be balanced against its readability. For infrequent mention in running text, it is suggested one refer to "the first and second beats of m. 36."

4.6. Rehearsal marks. Rehearsal marks—numbers or letters placed at selected locations in a score—are a convenient means of directing the reader to specific measures. The exact edition of the music in question needs to be made explicit to the reader, since rehearsal marks may differ from one edition to another. Use the word "rehearsal" followed by the appropriate number or letter enclosed in a box, such as $\boxed{10}$ or $\boxed{B}$. An alternate format is a number or letter in brackets: [10] or [B]. Locations before or after rehearsal marks may be written out, or may be indicated by a plus or minus sign and the number of measures in either direction. Explain this method to the reader when first used.

Observe the chord progression at rehearsal $\boxed{10}$ + 3
(three measures after rehearsal number 10).

The orchestra started the crescendo at rehearsal $\boxed{B}$ – 4.
or
The orchestra started the crescendo four measures before
rehearsal [B].

4.7. Systems. Another way of specifying sections of a score to the reader is to indicate a *system*. A system is two or more staves extending from the left margin to the right margin on the page, connected with a beginning brace and/or single bar lines. It is the musical analogue of a line of text. It is a visual indicator, not a musical one. Using this method, one needs to indicate the specific edition, the page number, the system number, and the measure number of that system counting from the left edge of the page. It is most likely used when no measure numbers are given, such as in original manuscripts or facsimiles. Abbreviations may be used if one employs this method extensively in an essay. For music written on only one staff (such as Bach's cello suites), one could use either the word "staff" or "system" in the designation.

> In the Smith edition of the quartet, notice the layout of
>   the C-major chord on page 3, system 2, measure 1.
> *or*
> . . . on p. 3, syst. 2, m. 1.

4.8. Time signatures. In running text, a time signature (or meter) may be written as a fraction with full-size baseline numerals (no superscripts or subscripts) separated by a slash, such as "4/4" or "6/8." Strictly speaking, time signatures are not fractions, so they would be written as one numeral directly over the other numeral without a slash or horizontal bar, as in a musical score; that is, $\frac{4}{4}$ and $\frac{6}{8}$. However, since other simple fractions would normally be written out in running text, there is little else that will be confused with a time signature expressed with a slash in a well-worded sentence.

> The meter changes to 3/4 three-quarters of the way through the piece.

There are several ways to express a time signature, all of which are acceptable. Occasionally the symbols C and ₵ may be used, especially if one is "quoting" the time signature of a specific piece. When mentioning "C" as a time signature, use bold type in a well-worded sentence so it is not misread as the note C. Do not spell out a time signature.

> The piece has a time signature of 9/8.
> The piece has a meter of 9/8.
> The piece is in 9/8 time.
> The piece is in 9/8 meter.
> The piece is in 9/8. (Use this form only when the topic of
>   meter is firmly established in the text.)

> Common time may be expressed as 4/4 or **C**.
> Cut time may be expressed as 2/2 or ₵.
> *not*
> This piece is in nine-eight meter.
> This piece is in four-quarter time.

4.9. Stops and registers. Organs and harpsichords have separate stops or registers that allow the performer to play not only at normal unison pitch, but at other pitch levels as well. Normal unison pitch for these instruments is referred to as "eight-foot" pitch, expressed just that way or as a number-plus-prime (8′). A register one octave above this has the designation "four-foot" (4′), and a register one octave below has the designation "sixteen-foot" (16′). The number-plus-prime format may be more appropriate if the text contains a considerable number of references to such pitch designations.

A single-manual harpsichord with two eight-foot registers is designated 2 × 8′, while a single-manual harpsichord with one eight-foot register and one four-foot register is designated 1 × 8′, 1 × 4′. A two-manual harpsichord with two eight-foot registers and one four-foot register is designated 2 × 8′, 1 × 4′, or, using roman numerals for the keyboards, as:

I: 1 × 8′, 1 × 4′
II: 1 × 8′
or
I: 8, 4   II: 8

Organ stops mentioned in running text have the foot designation followed by the stop name in capitalized roman type regardless of the language, such as 8′ Principal, 8′ Flûte harmonique, 4′ Rohrflöte, 4′ Roerfluit, and 2 2/3′ Quinte. This format is suggested in the interest of readability; that is, "8′ Principal" would be read as "eight-foot Principal." A compound stop with more than one rank has the stop name followed by the number of ranks in roman numerals, such as Mixture IV and Sesquialtera II. To improve readability of compound stops, they may also be referred to by division, such as "the Great Mixture" and "the Positive Cymbal." A recommended format for a stoplist is shown in table 4.1; principals and flutes are listed vertically from lowest to highest pitch, then compound stops, then reeds. Prime signs are omitted for a less cluttered look, and unit digits are aligned vertically.

A shorthand notation for a stoplist may be useful under some circumstances for saving space or for comparing different instruments. An example of such a notation is:

Gr: $16.8.8.4.2^{2}/_{3}.2.IV.8$
Pos: $8.4.4.2.1^{1}/_{3}.II.8$
P: $16.8.16$

Table 4.1. Representative Format for an Organ Stoplist

GREAT		POSITIVE		PEDAL	
16	Bourdon	8	Gedackt	16	Subbass
8	Principal	4	Principal	8	Principal
8	Rohrflöte	4	Rohrflöte	16	Posaune
4	Octave	2	Octave		
$2^2/_3$	Quinte	$1^1/_3$	Quinte		
2	Octave		Cymbal II		
	Mixture IV	8	Regal		
8	Trumpet				

Couplers: Pos/Gr   Gr/P   Pos/P
                 or, more accurately,
                 Pos→Gr   Gr→P   Pos→P

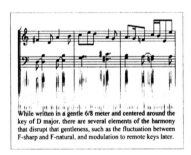

While written in a gentle 6/8 meter and centered around the key of D major, there are several elements of the harmony that disrupt that gentleness, such as the fluctuation between F-sharp and F-natural, and modulation to remote keys later.

5

Italic and Roman Type

5.1. Assimilation. For English text, it is generally recognized that non-English words or phrases are set in italic type (commonly referred to as "italics"). Since a great many musical terms are non-English, however, one could easily end up using too much italic type, thus making a sentence or even a page too "busy" and drawing attention to itself.

> In the final *tutti* of the *allegro* movement of the *concerto grosso*, the *continuo* player performed *con fuoco*, incorporating several *tirades*.

On the other hand, it has also been stated that italics are not used if a non-English word has been assimilated or incorporated into the English language, or if the word is familiar to readers. One indication of such assimilation is the appearance of the word in an English dictionary. While it cannot be said that all musical terms have reached this status, it certainly could be said that musical terms are assimilated and familiar at least within the context of a knowledgeable musician reading a text that is music-specific. Under these circumstances, it is better to follow the guideline of using roman type as much as possible and italics as little as possible in the interest of making a text less cluttered. The following discussion offers some guidelines.

5.2. Emphasis. Italics are used in any context if emphasis is needed. If the emphasis can be achieved without italics by rewording the sentence, use this approach, since overuse of italics diminishes its effectiveness.

> Stravinsky scored the piece for *eight* French horns.
> *may be rewritten*
> Stravinsky scored the piece for eight French horns, a number not often used.

5.3. First occurrence. If a non-English word is used repeatedly throughout a work, it may be italicized the first time it appears, then in roman type thereafter.

> This piece exemplifies the use of *scordatura*. Scordatura refers to . . .

5.4. German words. For German words there are considerations of both italics and capitalization, because of the German practice of capitalizing common nouns. In terms of italics, such terms may be italicized if used infrequently; but if used throughout an essay, follow the practice of italicizing the terms only at their first occurrence. In terms of capitalization, most terms should be left capitalized: *Augenmusik, Gebrauchsmusik, Musikwissenschaft, Schlaginstrument, Spielfreudigkeit*. Prominent examples that may be considered "more assimilated" than others are the terms *Lied, Singspiel*, and *Urtext*, which are thus more likely to appear not only in roman type but also lowercase. (Lowercase for German words would be considered an additional indication of assimilation into English.)

5.5. Instruments and genres. Names of instruments and genres are not italicized; use roman type regardless of the language. An exception would be when one is discussing the differences between country-specific instruments. Even in this instance, it may be possible to confine the use of italics to the first occurrence of the terms, and use roman type thereafter.

> The differences between the French *clavecin* and
> the German *Cembalo* are . . .

5.6. Performance terms. Use italics in running text for performance terms: dynamics, dynamic changes, tempo words when not titles, tempo changes, and instructions. This is based on the usage and recommendations in the majority of the style guides and references reviewed.

> Everyone was amazed at the violinist's *pianissimo*.
> Do not start the *crescendo* until m. 4.
> One person's *allegro* is another person's *presto*.
> The *accelerando* toward the end was very effective.
> The melody should be performed *cantabile*.

This italic rule would also apply when non-Italian terms are used: *ruhig bewegt* and *sehr lebhaft* in Hindemith's music, *assez animé et très rythmé* and *vif* in Debussy's music, *light and innocent* and *fast, rigid* in Leonard Bernstein's music. One must admit that some performance words are so familiar that, in a context in which they are used sparingly and are not referring to a specific musical example, roman type may be acceptable. However, if performance terms are used throughout an essay, use italics at all times for consistency.

> Legato is sometimes indicated by a slur.
> The repeated notes suggest a staccato treatment.

5.7. Tempo marking as title. If a piece has no other title and needs to be referred to by its tempo marking, that tempo marking becomes the title and so is capitalized and set in roman type. This assumes there is one overall marking for a movement; a piece that has many different tempo markings needs to be identified in another way.

> the Allegro molto from the Sonata no. 1
> the Maestoso from the Symphony no. 2
> *not*
> the Adagio/Allegro/Andante/Allegro/Presto from the Concerto no. 3

If the use of the tempo marking as a title is awkward—especially if it is in English—use an alternate means of identification.

> *instead of*
> the Calmly from the Sonata no. 3
> *use*
> the movement marked "Calmly" from the Sonata no. 3
> *or*
> the second movement from the Sonata no. 3

5.8. Avoiding ambiguity. Italics may be used to avoid confusion or ambiguity, such as the simultaneous use of a non-English word and an English word with the same spelling (but consider rewording the sentence).

> At the *a tempo* section, a tempo was selected that was faster
> than before.
> Even though the piece was originally written for harp, playing
> the passage *piano* on the piano was very effective.

5.9. Distinctions. Use italics to emphasize a distinction between certain words or musical concepts. Once the distinction has been made, roman type may be used thereafter.

> Two broad categories of clavichords are *fretted* and *unfretted*.
> Fretted clavichords are so named because . . .
> There are differences between the French *courante* and the Italian *corrente*. The courante is characterized by . . .

5.10. Non-English words and quotations marks. A word or phrase that would normally be italicized is set in roman type if it is enclosed in quotation marks, even if it is in a non-English language.

> the composer's use of *stile antico* in this work
> *but*
> the conductor wrote "stile antico" in the score

5.11. Incipits. Italics are not used for works that are identified by the first few words of text (incipits) even if in a non-English language, such as Bach's cantatas and chorale preludes. Rather, the text is in roman type and quotation marks. The quotation marks could be excluded if the title is part of a list of musical works, such as in a table.

> the cantata "Ein' feste Burg ist unser Gott," BWV 80
> "Öffne dich mein ganzes Herze" from Cantata no. 61

5.12. Example words. Other than the categories already mentioned—performance terms in italics, instruments and genres in roman type—table 5.1 gives examples of italic vs. roman type as found in the guides and references in the bibliography. This list is not comprehensive, only illustrative. Not every term in each category is universally found in that form in all sources. Some terms need only be italicized at their first occurrence.

The terms listed below were found to have inconsistent formats among the references: italicized in some references and in roman type in others. The discrepancies may be a consequence of different usages for the same term, or simply a matter of "house style." A brief discussion of each term is given as examples of how one may decide based on the guidelines already given here.

arioso. When used as a genre (a "small aria") it would be in roman type. When used as an indication of a piece in arioso style, it is also in

Table 5.1. Examples of Italic vs. Roman Type for Musical Terms

a cappella	*figura*	*pièce croisée*
agréments	*galant*	*port de voix*
alla breve	*intermedio*	*ritournelle*
alternatim	*lauda*	*sonata da camera*
ballet de cour	*mâitre de chappelle*	*sonata da chiesa*
bariolage	*manualiter*	*stile antico*
basso seguente	*musica ficta*	*style brisé*
bel canto	*notes inégales*	*style galant*
col arco	*opera buffa*	*sul ponticello*
col legno	*opéra comique*	*sul tasto*
comédie-ballet	*opera seria*	*tactus*
détaché	*ouverture*	*tirade*
double	*pedaliter*	*tirata*
en rondeau	*perpetuum mobile*	*una corda*
alto	continuo	portamento
appoggiatura	da capo aria	quodlibet
arpeggio	dal segno aria	ripieno
avant-garde	falsetto	ritornello
basso continuo	frottola	rondeau
bicinium	glissando	scordatura
cadenza	libretto	soprano
castrato	oeuvre	stretto
clausula	opus	tessitura
coda	organum	tremolo
coloratura	ostinato	tutti
concerto grosso	pizzicato	vibrato

roman type, with the word "style" specifically used. When used as a performance term, it would be italicized ("the middle section was labeled *arioso cantabile*").

ballade. This refers to several types of musical works (one of the three *formes fixes*; a narrative poem or song in German; piano works of Chopin, Liszt, and Brahms) but since they are all compositions, the term would be lowercase roman type when used as a genre, capitalized roman type when used as a specific title.

Cammerton, Chorton. These are both capitalized German nouns; retaining the capitalization is suggested. If used rarely, italicize them. Otherwise, italicize at their first occurrence and use roman type thereafter.

cantus firmus. This term is evenly split in the references: half use italics, half use roman type. The case for roman type is that the term does not resemble any English words and would never be confused with any other term.

conductus. This is a genre, and so would be in roman type, but italicizing its first occurrence would alert the reader.

da capo, dal segno. If used as part of a genre—da capo aria, dal segno aria—use roman type. If used in other contexts—such as a discussion of ornaments added to a *da capo* section—italics may be used.

divertissement. If used as a genre (like divertimento), use roman type. If used as a French word in a French context, use italics.

entrée. This term may be used as a genre term, but it also has many subtle meanings and does not seem to be an assimilated term. Use italics.

fauxbourdon. This term can be used in roman type (italicized at its first appearance) if it is the main topic of an essay. If being used in a context in which it is necessary to distinguish it from similar terms—falsobordone, faburden—italics may prove useful.

obbligato. This is seen so often it probably should be considered an assimilated term. Use roman type.

5.13. Word as word. When one discusses a word as a word—for example, the four-letter term "oboe" and not the woodwind instrument so named—the word may be either italicized or in roman type and quotation marks. Many style guides opt for italics, but just as many accept either option. Sometimes the selection of one practice over another may be a subtle distinction as to how the sentence looks, or may simply be personal preference. In the first two pairs of example sentences that follow, either format seems appropriate. (It should be mentioned that the guidelines that the word "sonata" as a genre would normally be in roman type and the word "cantabile" as a performance term would normally be in italics are overruled by the current guideline.) In the third pair of sentences, the use of italics may have the advantage of producing a less cluttered look. (See another example of this in section 5.4.)

Both D. Scarlatti and Mozart used the term *sonata*.
or
Both D. Scarlatti and Mozart used the term "sonata."

My teacher wrote the word *cantabile* in m. 79.
or
My teacher wrote the word "cantabile" in m. 79.

In his keyboard partitas, Bach used six different names for the
preludes: *Praeludium, Sinfonia, Fantasia, Ouverture,*
Praeambulum, and *Toccata.*
or
In his keyboard partitas, Bach used six different names for the
preludes: "Praeludium," "Sinfonia," "Fantasia," "Ouverture,"
"Praeambulum," and "Toccata."

In some contexts, quotation marks carry subtle meanings. Their use
in the first sentence below implies the definition of the word is being
stretched. Their use in the second sentence is because it is a direct
quote, but may imply the writer does not agree with the reviewer.

Two notes of the same pitch form the "interval" of a unison.
The reviewer believed the sound of the violin was "anemic."

The word-as-word format may also be different for different circumstances. In the first example below, the word "allemande" is in
roman type without quotation marks because it is a genre and because it
is being referred to as a musical form, not as a term. In the second sentence, the word is in italics (breaking the genre-in-roman rule) because
(1) it needs to be singled out since it is being referred to as a term, and
(2) the translation of the word in the same sentence is in quotation
marks. The different modes of emphasis for the different functions of
each word seem logical. In the third sentence, it is in roman type and
quotation marks because italics would put the format and the meaning
of the sentence at odds.

Many Baroque suites begin with an allemande.
The term *allemande* is the French word for "German."
Genre terms such as "allemande" are not italicized.

An example of suspending a rule for a particular reason may be
seen in section 7.4. There the question of plurals of non-English terms
is discussed and all terms that are given as illustrations are in roman
type.

6

Compound Words and Hyphenation

6.1. Compound word types. The use of two or more words to represent a single item or idea presents the problem of how they should be expressed in running text. Three forms are: (1) an *open compound word*, written as separate words ("lower case"); (2) a *hyphenated compound word*, separated by a hyphen ("lower-case"); and (3) a *closed compound word*, written as one word ("lowercase").

6.2. General compounding rules. To help determine which compound word type is appropriate for a given situation, two sources are suggested. The first is a list of suggested rules for forming compound words as found in a comprehensive style guide such as *The Chicago Manual of Style* or the *United States Government Printing Office Style Manual* (see bibliography). The second is how compound words are listed in an English-language dictionary or a music dictionary. Unfortunately, after reviewing the references in the bibliography, it is apparent that there is a wide diversity of guidelines to the point that one can find conflicting usage among the many style guides and even inconsistent usage within a given style guide. The following selected rules—predominantly from the *United States Government Printing Office Style Manual*—are offered as starting points for approaching the use of compound words in a musical context.

6.2.1. Two-term compound words. A hyphen is not necessary for two-term compound words when its omission does not cause ambiguity in the sense of the term or in the way it sounds.

concert hall	piano tuner	tone poem
key signature	song cycle	treble clef

6.2.2. Three-term compound words. A hyphen is not necessary for three-term compound words when the meaning is clear and the term "reads" well.

diminished seventh chord   music school curriculum
harmonic minor scale   song cycle composer
minor key signature   third harmonic frequency

6.2.3. Confusing modifiers. Use a hyphen to avoid any confusion between a modifier and the word it modifies. For extended multi-word modifiers, consider rewording the sentence.

modern-music dictionary *vs.* modern music dictionary
old-record collector *vs.* old record collector
two-piano concertos *vs.* two piano concertos
whole-note sequence *vs.* whole note sequence

a northern Italian early Baroque violin maker
may be rewritten
a violin maker working in northern Italy during the early
    Baroque era

6.2.4. Repeated letters. Use a hyphen to avoid a double vowel or a triple consonant. There are exceptions to this, but some of the exceptions are listed as both closed and hyphenated in certain dictionaries.

anti-impressionistic
de-emphasize
trill-like
pre-eminent *or* preeminent
re-examine *or* reexamine
cooperation *not* co-operation
coordinated *not* co-ordinated

6.2.5. Ambiguity. Use a hyphen to avoid mispronunciation, to ensure a definite accent, or to avoid ambiguity. Consider inserting a hyphen for clarity even if the dictionary does not (as in the case of "over-age").

even-ing (smoothing out) *vs.* evening (time of day)
over-age (too old) *vs.* overage (excess)
pre-concert (before a concert) *vs.* preconcert (arrange in advance)
pre-position (place in advance) *vs.* preposition (part of speech)
re-petition (petition again) vs. repetition (restatement)
re-sent (sent again) *vs.* resent (feel displeasure)
re-sign (sign again) *vs.* resign (give up)
re-solve (solve again) *vs.* resolve (settle; chord resolution)

6.2.6. Closed compound word. A compound word is closed when the idea or concept it conveys is different from the meanings of the separated words. A closed compound word is often characterized by one primary accent and a prefixed term with one syllable.

| downbeat | hornpipe | meantone |
| footnote | keyboard | plainsong |

6.2.7. Sound pattern. Compared to an open compound word, a closed compound word tends to have a different sound pattern based on the stress of the syllables. So, the way a compound word is pronounced may give a clue to how it may be written.

That piece of wood is a sound board. (sound′ board′)
The artist is decorating the soundboard. (sound′board)

The key to the door is on the key board. (key′ board′)
The builder finished making the keyboard. (key′board)

That is a rather plain song. (plain′ song′)
The choir performed plainsong. (plain′song)

6.2.8. Open vs. hyphenated vs. closed. A general—but not strict—tendency is for a compound word to go from open to hyphenated to closed the longer it is established in the language. However, words such as the following have been found in all three configurations concurrently among different references, and even within a given style guide. This guideline applies to words that represent the same part of speech, because some terms change their configuration depending on their usage. For example, "carry over" as a verb is open, while "carry-over" as a noun is hyphenated.

lower case, lower-case, lowercase
on line, on-line, online
organ building, organ-building, organbuilding

6.3. Musical elements. For the names of musical elements—notes, intervals, chords, scales, and clefs, as nouns—use an open configuration. Some selected modifiers, however, need to be hyphenated.

eighth note
dotted eighth note, *but* double-dotted eighth note

quarter tone
major third (interval)
major chord
sixth chord, *but* six-four chord
diminished seventh chord, *but* half-diminished seventh chord
major scale
harmonic minor scale
G clef
treble clef

6.4. Ordinal abbreviations. Some writers use abbreviations for compound words when referring to chords and intervals with ordinal numbers, such as "diminished 7th chord" and "the interval of a major 3rd." However, abbreviations should be avoided in running text. While these abbreviations may help clarify some sentences with double ordinals, it is better to reword the sentence or avoid double ordinals altogether. Abbreviations may be used in tables to save space.

not
The eighth note is an eighth note.
but
By counting notes, the eighth one in the melody has the
    value of an eighth note.
not
The seventh chord is the seventh chord.
but
In m. 24, the chord on the second beat is a seventh chord.

6.5. Prefixes. Words that begin with a prefix are generally closed, but use a hyphen before numerals, capitalized words, and repeated letters.

anticlimactic
neoclassical
nonharmonic, nonmusical, *but* non-English
postimpressionism, *but* post-1900, post-Stravinsky
premodern, *but* pre-1600, pre-Baroque
subdominant, submediant, *but* sub-baritone
supertonic, *but* super-rhythmic

6.6. Multiple hyphens. For terms with multiple hyphens, an en dash may be substituted for a hyphen when one of the terms is an open compound word or a hyphenated compound word. If the structure of the term with multiple hyphens becomes too complicated, consider rewriting the sentence.

dotted–eighth-note pattern
early–eighteenth-century music
post–Baroque era concerto

not
a double-dotted–eighth-note pattern
but
a pattern of double-dotted eighth notes

6.7. Centuries. The following formats are recommended for referring to time periods.

of the early eighteenth century
of the mid-eighteenth century
early–eighteenth-century music
mid–eighteenth-century music

6.8. Compound words as adjectives. An open compound word becomes hyphenated when used as an adjective or modifier.

an eighth note, *but* an eighth-note pattern
a dotted eighth note, *but* a dotted–eighth-note pattern
the key of C major, *but* a C-major scale
a range of two octaves, *but* a two-octave range
     (note the singular form of "octave")

6.9. Example words. The following lists present examples of compound words in various forms. These are admittedly selective lists. The words in the categories "open," "hyphenated," and "closed" are those terms in which *The New Harvard Dictionary of Music* and *Grove Music Online* agree; the variable category contains words in which those references disagree (with the most common difference being the British convention of liberal hyphenation). In addition, the words are given a score based on the OneLook® Dictionary Search (see bibliography), which examines the entries from a multitude of reference sources. The score lists the number of dictionary entries giving a term as either open (O), hyphenated (H), closed (C), or a combination thereof. For example, "O7" means seven references list the term as an open compound; "OH1" means one reference lists the term as both open and hyphenated. This list should not be considered immutable; there is the possibility of different usage in some circumstances. For example, in much of the organ-related literature, the words "organbuilding" and "windchest" are often closed.

Open	OneLook®
chin rest	O7
cut time	O5
double bar	O11
double bass	O12, OH7
double stop	O3, H5, OH1
double tongue	O5, H7, OH1
organ building	H1
part song	O8, H2, C6
song cycle	O6
tone color	O9
tone poem	O16
tone row	O9
tune book	—
tuning pin	O1

Hyphenated	OneLook®
double-time	O7, H1, OH4
down-bow	H11
mezzo-forte	O8, H1
mezzo-soprano	OH1, H17
sight-reading	O1, H4, OH 1
up-bow	H10
wind-chest	O2, C2

Closed	OneLook®
concertgoer	H8, C6
concertmaster	O1, C8, CH1
countermelody	H1, C5
countersubject	C4
countertenor	O3, H1, C19, OH1
downbeat	O1, C16
fingerboard	O2, H1, C19
hornpipe	C22
kettledrum	O1, H2, C25, OH1
keyboard	C52
mouthpiece	O1, C31
overtone	C34

partbook	C1
pedalboard	O1, C2
pipework	C7
plainchant	O3, H1, C14
plainsong	O3, H1, C19, OH1
soundboard	O1, H5, C12
upbeat	H1, C20

Variable	*HDM*	*GMO*	*OneLook®*
bar line	O	H	O9, OC1
counter fugue	C	H	—
cross rhythm	O	H	H1
folk song	O	C	O15, C6
mean tone	C	H	OH1
off beat	C	H	O1, H2, C19, OH1
part writing	O	H	—
sound hole	O	C	O10, C1
tuning fork	O	H	O23, H1

6.10. Word division

6.10.1. General considerations. Word division or end-line hyphenation—the separation of a multi-syllable word between two lines of text by means of a hyphen at the right margin—is a necessity because of the dual requirements in a publication of a justified right edge of text and proper word spacing. The primary guide for determining where a word may be divided is the dictionary. However, some musical terms and concepts would not be found in a regular dictionary, and many music dictionaries do not provide hyphenation. The following guidelines for word division are based on the references in the bibliography, but it should be understood that there is no definitive method of hyphenating words. Even though many publishers expressly mention not to break words during manuscript preparation—that is, the document should have an unjustified right margin and no end-line hyphenation— familiarity with the rules is important for publishers during page preparation and for authors during proofreading. One should not rely exclusively on the hyphenation option of a word processor.

6.10.2. Single-syllable words. The *-ed* form of a one-syllable word is still considered a one-syllable word and is not divided.

| bowed | played | stringed | trilled |

6.10.3. Initial single letter. Do not use divisions that leave a single letter at the end of a line.

a-dagio   A-madeus   e-vensong   I-talian

6.10.4. Letters to second line. Divide a word so that no fewer than three letters go to the second line. This rule is sometimes suspended when a two-letter syllable on the second line is followed by a punctuation mark (period, comma, colon, semicolon, question mark).

an-dante, *not* andan-te   im-promptu, *not* impromp-tu
com-poser, *not* compos-er   so-nata, *not* sona-ta

6.10.5. Number of letters. Do not divide words of four letters or less. Words of five letters may be divided if at least two letters are left at the end of a line and three letters go to the second line.

do not divide
Dei, Deo, duo, era, Ian, Ite, più, una
Aïda, alto, aria, coda, *Lulu*, oboe, opus, solo, trio
cel-lo, Chlo-é, é-tude, gen-re, Hay-dn, mez-zo, ton-al, vi-o-la
divide if necessary
ma-jor, mi-nor, mu-sic, op-era, vo-cal

6.10.6. Misread words. Avoid dividing words that might be misread even when divided correctly.

Cop-land   rear-range

6.10.7. Pronunciation vs. derivation. Divide according to pronunciation rather than word derivation or etymology. This is a feature of United States English as opposed to British English; the latter often takes derivation into account. (Note that not all division points are given here.)

antiph-onal, *not* anti-phonal, *but* anti-phon
bibliog-raphy, *not* biblio-graphy, *but* biblio-graphical
discog-raphy, *not* disco-graphy
musi-cian, *not* music-ian
musi-cology, *not* music-ology
orga-nology, *not* organ-ology
polyph-ony, *not* poly-phony, *but* poly-phonic

One will encounter some problems with this guideline. First, it is sometimes difficult to determine to which syllable a letter belongs; that is, a letter may be shared phonetically with two adjacent syllables. For example, with the word *performance* the letter *m* could be considered part of either the second or third syllable. As a consequence, one can find it divided "per-for-mance" in some dictionaries and "per-form-ance" in others. Another such word is *measure* ("mea-sure" or "meas-ure"). Second, the existence of multiple but equally acceptable pronunciations means that a word may be divided more than one way. In instances like these, it may have to be admitted that either division is acceptable.

Word	Pronunciation	Hyphenation
pianist	pee'-uh-nist	pia-nist
	pee-an'-ist	pian-ist
prelude	pray'-lood, pree'-lood	pre-lude
	prel'-yood	prel-ude

6.10.8. Single middle vowel. When a vowel forms a syllable in the middle of a word, include it in the first line if possible. An exception to this is a word with a prefix.

clavi-chord, *not* clav-ichord
dimi-nution, *not* dim-inution
hexa-chord, *not* hex-achord
idio-phone, *not* idi-ophone
manu-script, *not* man-uscript
tempera-ment, *not* temper-ament
varia-tion, *not* vari-ation
vio-lin, *not* vi-olin
but
un-even, *not* une-ven
un-opened, *not* uno-pened

6.10.9. Hyphenated words. Divide hyphenated words after the hyphen.

composer-/performer   down-/bow   mezzo-/soprano

6.10.10. Closed compound words. Divide closed compound words at the natural break.

concert/master   counter/subject   forte/piano

6.10.11. Gerunds and participles. Divide most gerunds and present participles before the *ing*. If the final consonant before the *ing* is doubled, the division is between the consonants. Exceptions to this last rule are words that have their own double consonant such as *trill* and *miss*.

> compos-ing, finger-ing, play-ing
> hum-ming, run-ning
> trill-ing, miss-ing

6.10.12. Usage-dependent hyphenation. Some words change hyphenation depending on usage, the basis of which in most cases is a different pronunciation.

> in′-va-lid (noun) *vs.* in-val′-id (adjective)
> min′-ute (noun) *vs.* mi-nute′ (adjective)
> pres′-ent (noun, adjective) *vs.* pre-sent′ (verb)
> proj′-ect (noun) *vs.* pro-ject′ (verb)
> rec′-ord (noun) *vs.* re-cord′ (verb)
> out-of-tune notes (adjective) *vs.* playing out of tune (adverb)

6.10.13. Different pronunciation, same hyphenation. Some words have different pronunciations for the same spelling and hyphenation. When such words are hyphenated, there is the possibility that they may be misread.

> con′-cert (noun) *vs.* con-cert′ (verb)
> con′-duct (noun) *vs.* con-duct′ (verb)
> con′-test (noun) *vs.* con-test′ (verb)
> per′-fect (adjective) *vs.* per-fect′ (verb)
> sub′-ject (noun) *vs.* sub-ject′ (verb)

6.10.14. Large terms. Alphanumeric terms and large numerals should be left intact. To avoid a break, reword the sentence.

> The instrument's catalog number is
> HD7-PT1769.15

> The current edition of the dictionary contains over 300,000 words.

> The hyphenation of names is discussed in section
> 6.10.22.

6.10.15. Abbreviations. Do not divide an acronym, an initialism, or an abbreviation with numerals.

do not divide

K. 385	A440	D.M.A.
m. 79	523 Hz	ca. 1750

divide if necessary
BWV / 1048

6.10.16. Lists. When enumerating items in running text, do not separate the designations (1), (2), (3) or (a), (b), (c) from the item being enumerated at the end of a line. The exception is when one is not giving a list but is describing the format itself, as in the preceding sentence.

not
Compound words may be either (1)
open; (2) hyphenated; or (3) closed.
rather
Compound words may be either
(1) open; (2) hyphenated; or (3) closed.
but
Do not separate the designations (1),
(2), (3) or (a), (b), (c) . . .

6.10.17. Internet addresses. For uniform resource locators (URLs) and e-mail addresses, do not introduce a hyphen that is not part of the original address. Do not break at an existing hyphen. Breaks should be *after* a colon, slash, double slash, or the symbol @, but *before* a period or other punctuation or symbol. If a very long element must be broken, try to break it between word units.

http://	http://www	http://www.m-w
www.m-w.com	.m-w.com	.com

not
http://www.m-
w.com

http://www.grove   *not*   http://www.grove-
music.com   music.com

http://areditions.com/mla/notes/
stylesheet.html

http://assets.cambridge.org/ECM/ECM
_ifc.pdf

musiceditor@
bookpublisher.com

6.10.18. Musical elements. Do not divide keys, clef names, or pitches.

| G clef | E-flat | G♯ |
| C-G | D-F♯-A | $C\text{–}d^3$ |

D major (*but if necessary* B-flat / major)
middle C (*but if necessary* mid/dle C)

6.10.19. Non-English words. For division of non-English words, look for them in the dictionary, refer to the guidelines in a comprehensive style guide, or consult an expert in the language. Another clue is to find a related word in an English dictionary. One can also try to avoid dividing them. A useful reference that may offer clues to hyphenation is Iowa State University's *Pronouncing Dictionary of Music and Musicians* (see bibliography). In most European languages, words may be divided between consonants, or after a vowel and before the next consonant. For German compound words, pay attention to the component parts of the word; they may not necessarily divide between doubled letters. One suggestion is "anglicized hyphenation"—using English hyphenation rules even for non-English languages—but be aware that the results may look wrong to someone familiar with the original language. (In the examples given below, note that some division points are not given, particularly those that leave two final letters.)

Also sprach Za-ra-thus-tra
Les bar-ri-cades mis-té-rieuses
Ca-val-le-ria rus-ti-cana
La Ce-ne-ren-tola
di-min-u-endo (cf. English di-min-u-tive)
di-ver-tisse-ment
Trois Gym-no-pé-dies
I Pa-gliacci
Quo-ti-es-cun-que man-du-ca-bi-tis
Le quat-tro sta-gioni
sin-fo-nietta (cf. English sym-pho-ny)

Stimm-stock
Das wohl-tem-pe-rirte Cla-vier

6.10.20. Non-English open compound words. Do not divide non-English open compound words when the first term has only one to three letters.

a cappella	*ad libitum*	*dal segno*
a tempo	*da capo*	*sul tasto*

6.10.21. Personal names: Dividing without hyphens. For personal names of more than one element—first name, middle name, last name, initials, etc.—divide between the elements. Divide after an existing hyphen. A name with a single first initial—used to differentiate members of a family such as Couperin or Scarlatti—should not be divided after the initial. Divide a name with a middle initial after that initial; multiple middle initials may be divided before the initials if necessary. Avoid a break before a name suffix (Jr., Sr., II, III).

Hans T. / David
Manuel / de Falla
Ralph / Vaughan / Williams
E. Power / Biggs, *not* E. / Power Biggs
Johann / Strauss Jr., *not* Johann Strauss / Jr.
Arthur W. J. G. / Ord-Hume (*if necessary* Arthur / W. J. G.)
Wolfgang / Alexander / Thomas-/San-/Galli
do not divide
D. / Scarlatti   G. / Silbermann   J. S. / Bach   B. B. / King
divide if necessary
C. P. E. / Bach   Mrs. H. H. A. / Beach

6.10.22. Personal names: Dividing with hyphens. In terms of end-line hyphenation, one can avoid dividing names, but this approach may be unrealistic for longer names. If a name is found in the dictionary, use that hyphenation. Otherwise, the following guidelines are offered.

1. Divide at an existing hyphen (Karg-/Elert, Marc-/Antoine, Saint-/Saëns, Villa-/Lobos).
2. Divide according to a name's obvious components, often between two different consonants (Arm-strong, Bern-stein, Schoen-berg, Tuck-well, Vieux-temps). This is especially useful for names with three

syllables when one of the division points is ambiguous or variable due to different pronunciations. For example, the name "Horowitz" may be found in the references as both "Ho-ro-witz" and "Hor-o-witz." In this instance, use "Horo-witz." Similarly, use Boro-din, Casa-vant, Cléram-bault, Friede-mann, Tele-mann, and Vladi-mir.

3. Divide according to pronunciation (Cho-pin, Du-kas, Jo-hann, Schu-bert). Be aware that some names spelled the same way have different hyphenations in other languages because of different pronunciations, such as Rob-ert (English) vs. Ro-bert (French and German), or Rich-ard (English) vs. Ri-chard (German). A useful reference for pronunciation is Iowa State University's *Pronouncing Dictionary of Music and Musicians* (see bibliography) from which hyphenation may be deduced.

4. Divide after a vowel and before a consonant (Ma-yu-zu-mi, Pa-ga-ni-ni, Stra-di-va-ri). Generally, treat two consecutive vowels as a single vowel (Cha-lia-pin, Dia-ghi-lev, Joa-chim, Leo-pold, Sa-lie-ri, Scria-bin).

5. Divide between a doubled consonant, especially when a vowel is on each side (Brit-ten, Chaus-son, Mes-siaen, Ros-sini, Wil-liams, Zim-mer). The main exception to this is German names with triple consonants, two of which are doubled; these may not divide at the doubled consonant (Bamm-ler, Hoff-mann, Kell-ner).

6. If a name has an equivalent common word in the dictionary, use that hyphenation (ba-con, bar-ber, car-pen-ter, dia-mond, hol-i-day, pis-ton, sar-gent, shep-herd, tay-lor). If a last name is identical to a common first name, these might also be found in the dictionary (Ar-nold, Ben-nett, Her-man, Law-rence, Mar-tin, Ste-vens). Otherwise, a close equivalent found in the dictionary may give a clue, providing the pronunciation of the English word is not too dissimilar to the name.

Name	*Close Equivalent*
Char-pen-tier	car-pen-ter
Grain-ger	stran-ger
Har-ri-son	gar-ri-son
Klem-per-er	em-per-or
Or-man-dy	Nor-man-dy
Prae-to-ri-us	prae-to-ri-an
Ra-vel	re-veal (*not* rav′-el)
Tar-ti-ni	mar-ti-ni

The following highly selective list offers examples of how personal names may be divided. Again, one will find discrepancies among the references that are related to differences in pronunciation; for example: Ho-ro-witz // Hor-o-witz, Me-nu-hin // Men-u-hin, Oi-strakh // Ois-trakh, Pro-ko-fi-ev // Pro-kof-iev, and Vla-di-mir // Vlad-i-mir. Not all division points are given; some are excluded because they violate one of the previous guidelines (do not divide words of fewer than four letters; do not leave a single letter at the end of a line; do not leave fewer than three letters at the beginning of a line, do not carry a single middle vowel to the second line). A hyphen (-) indicates a suggested acceptable break between syllables. An en dash (–) is used as a substitute for an existing hyphen in the interest of clarity, to differentiate it from a breaking hyphen. A slash (/) is used to avoid ambiguity in indicating the location of an acceptable break. Be aware that some legitimate hyphenations may cause problems with misreading; for example, "De-" with Debussy, "Bee-" with Beethoven, and "Cop-" with Copland.

Anony-mous	Claude De-bussy
Louis Arm-strong	Léo De-libes
Vladi-mir Ash-ke-nazy	Fred-er-ick De-lius
Anna Mag-de-lena Bach	Ser-gei Dia-ghi-lev
Carl Phi-lipp Ema-nuel Bach	Vin-cent d'Indy
Jo-hann Se-bas-tian Bach	Ernst von Doh-ná-nyi
Wil-helm Frie-de-mann Bach	Paul Du-kas
Béla Bar-tók	An-to-nín Dvo-řák
Lud-wig van Bee-tho-ven	Ma-nuel de Falla
Hec-tor Ber-lioz	Ga-briel Fauré
Georges Bi-zet	José Fe-li-ciano
Luigi Boc-che-rini	Lu-do-vico Fo-gliano
Al-ex-an-der Bo-ro-din	Ru-dolf Friml
Jo-han-nes Brahms	Gio-vanni Ga-bri-eli
An-ton Bruck-ner	George Gersh-win
Die-terich Bux-te-hude	Mi-khail Glinka
En-rico Ca-ruso	Louis Mo-reau Gott-schalk
Ma-rio	Charles Gou-nod
Cas-tel-nuovo–/Tedesco	Ni-co-las de Gri-gny
Jacques Cham-pion	George Fri-de-ric Han-del
Cham-bon-nières	Franz Jo-seph Haydn
Marc–/Antoine Char-pen-tier	Hans Wer-ner Henze
Fré-dé-ric Cho-pin	Paul Hin-de-mith
Mu-zio Cle-menti	Hugo von Hof-manns-thal
Fran-çois Cou-pe-rin	Bil-lie Holi-day

Ar-thur Ho-neg-ger
Vladi-mir Horo-witz
Alan Ho-vha-ness
Mi-khail
    Ip-po-li-tov–/Ivanov
Leoš Ja-ná-ček
Jo-seph Joa-chim
Dmi-tri Ka-ba-lev-sky
Is-rael Ka-ma-ka-wi-wo'ole
Sig-frid Karg–/Elert
Aram Kha-cha-tu-rian
Zol-tán Ko-dály
Serge Kous-se-vitzky
Ernst Kře-nek
Gus-tav Mah-ler
To-shirō Ma-yu-zumi
Fe-lix Men-dels-sohn
Ye-hudi Menu-hin
Oli-vier Mes-siaen
Ar-turo Be-ne-detti
    Mi-chel-an-geli
Wolf-gang Ama-deus
    Mo-zart
Mo-dest Mus-sorg-sky
Bir-git Nils-son
Jo-han-nes Ocke-ghem
Da-vid Oi-strakh
Nic-colò Pa-ga-nini
Gio-vanni Pier-luigi da
    Pa-le-strina
Krzysz-tof Pen-de-recki
Vin-cent Per-si-chetti
Mi-chael Prae-to-rius

Ser-gei Pro-ko-fiev
Ser-gei Rach-ma-ni-noff
Mau-rice Ra-vel
Ot-to-rino Re-spi-ghi
Ni-ko-lai
    Rim-sky–/Kor-sa-kov
Gio-ac-chino Ros-sini
Msti-slav Ros-tro-po-vich
Gen-nady Rozh-dest-ven-sky
Esa–/Pekka Sa-lo-nen
Do-me-nico Scar-latti
Pe-ter Schick-ele
Ar-nold Schoen-berg
Franz Schu-bert
Ro-bert Schu-mann
Alex-an-der Scria-bin
Dmi-tri Sho-sta-ko-vich
Jean Si-be-lius
Be-dřich Sme-tana
An-to-nio Stra-di-vari
Igor Stra-vin-sky
Fer-ruc-cio Ta-glia-vini
Pe-ter Il-yich Tchai-kov-sky
Alex-an-der Tche-rep-nin
Ge-org Phi-lipp Te-le-mann
Ralph Vaughan Wil-liams
Giu-seppe Verdi
Hei-tor Villa–/Lobos
An-to-nio Vi-valdi
Ri-chard Wag-ner
Carl Ma-ria von Weber
An-ton We-bern
Eu-gène Ysaÿe

7

Word Forms

7.1. Abbreviations

7.1.1. Types. There are several distinct forms of condensed words and phrases. An *acronym* is a series of first letters that is pronounceable as a word (ASCAP, MIDI). An *initialism* is a series of first letters that is read as letters (BWV, GFA). A *contraction* is a shortened form of a word that eliminates one or more interior letters, and often contains only the first and last letters (ca. for circa, Hz for hertz, no. for number from the Latin "numero"). An *abbreviation* is typically a truncated form of a word (op. for opus, vol. for volume) but may also used for those that fit no other category. For simplicity, the word "abbreviation" will sometimes be used as the uniform title for all these types collectively.

7.1.2. Acceptable abbreviations. Avoid abbreviations in running text. Too many abbreviations, especially unfamiliar ones, may be obtrusive or frustrating to the reader. Several familiar exceptions for music-related writing are listed below. Other abbreviations should be reserved for tables and citations, or when quoting a specific phrase. Unfortunately, there does not seem to be a definitive list of musical abbreviations; for example, the abbreviation for "violin" has been given variously as V., v., vio, vl, vln, and vn. Another problem is that some references list abbreviations always capitalized and always followed by a period, and it is difficult to determine if these are integral to the abbreviation itself or just the way the text was formatted. If abbreviations are to be used, use as few as possible, give preference to familiar ones, select those that are unambiguous within the given context, and inform the reader what the abbreviations mean.

BWV, K., etc.	catalog designations
ca.	circa
dB	decibels (may be written out)
Hz	hertz (may be written out)

m., mm.	measure, measures
M. M.	Maelzel metronome
no., nos.	number, numbers (designating a piece)
op., opp.	opus, opera or opuses (designating a piece)
rpm	revolutions per minute (*not* "rpms")

BWV 80	M. M. = 90
ca. 1700	Partita no. 5
72 dB *or* 72 decibels	op. 34, nos. 1 and 2
415 Hz *or* 415 hertz	opp. 19 and 25
m. 1, mm. 24–26	78 rpm record

not
a large no. of concertos
the Beethoven op. list
several mm. long
but
The designation "à 2 Clav. et Ped." was at the top of the manuscript.

7.1.3. Performance terms. In musical scores, abbreviations are used for dynamics (*pp, p, mp, mf, f, ff*), dynamic changes (*cresc., decresc.*), tempo changes (*accel., rall.*), and performance indications (*stacc., ten.*). When referring to these terms in running text, spell them out fully. The exception is when one is discussing the abbreviations themselves.

Notice that the right hand part is marked *piano* and the
     left hand part is marked *forte.*
There is a *crescendo* in m. 32 of the original score.
The designation for "left hand" may be "l.h.", "m.g.", or "m.s."

7.1.4. Initial abbreviation. Do not start a sentence with an abbreviation, even an acceptable one.

Measures 79–83 contain . . .	Opus 67 demonstrates . . .
not	*not*
Mm. 79–83 contain . . .	Op. 67 demonstrates . . .

Circa 1700, . . .
or
About 1700, . . .
not
Ca. 1700, . . .

7.1.5. Acronyms and initialisms. An entire name or title should be written out at its first occurrence and the acronym or initialism given parenthetically immediately following, in unspaced uppercase letters without periods. Some guides recommend using italics for non-English acronyms and for terms that would normally be italicized if spelled out, such as the title of a book. However, this practice varies. Some references suggest that since acronyms are pronounceable, they should be written as words, by analogy with the terms "laser" and "radar"; so, for example, ASCAP becomes "Ascap" and MIDI becomes "midi." Again, this practice varies. If the size of capital letters seems obtrusive and out of proportion to the rest of the text, small caps or a smaller font size may be used (ASCAP instead of ASCAP).

American Society of Composers, Authors, and Publishers (ASCAP)
Bach Werke Verzeichnis (BWV)
Guitar Foundation of America (GFA)
musical instrument digital interface (MIDI)
one voice per part (OVPP)
Société Suisse de Musicologie (SSM)
Das wohltemperirte Clavier or *The Well-Tempered Clavier* (WTC)

7.1.6. New acronyms and initialisms. For titles or concepts mentioned throughout an essay, new acronyms or initialisms may be devised.

A History of Western Music (HWM)
invertible counterpoint (IC)
on period instruments (OPI)

However, extensive use of non-standard acronyms or initialisms in running text may frustrate the reader; they may be most helpful when an essay deals with repeated references to a few items. Use them if they are easily grasped and they vastly assist the reader. For example, a discussion of American vs. British English might use "AmE" and "BrE" while a discussion of the *Brandenburg Concertos* might refer to them as "BC1," "BC2," "BC3," and so on.

7.2. Capitalization

7.2.1. Rules. Complete rules for capitalization, including non-English phrases, may be found in comprehensive style guides (see bibliography).

7.2.2. Numbered items. In running text, words or abbreviations referring to a numbered item are lowercase (but see section 2.27).

found in chapter 1   in act 2, scene 3
shown in figure 2   Symphony no. 1
presented in table 3   Sonata op. 27, no. 2
as seen in example 4

7.2.3. Scales. Scales that are designated with a descriptive name rather than a note name are lowercase.

chromatic scale   minor scale
harmonic minor scale   pentatonic scale
major scale   whole-tone scale

7.2.4. Assimilated non-English words. Non-English words that are usually capitalized in the original language (especially German) are lowercase if they have been assimilated into English. This practice, however, varies.

lied   singspiel   urtext

7.2.5. Historical periods. Periods of musical history are capitalized but the same words used in other contexts as modifiers are lowercase.

Gothic   Classical, Classicism
Renaissance   Romantic, Romanticism
Baroque

but
a gothic setting (meaning medieval)
a renaissance of chamber music (meaning renewed interest)
the baroque elements of the organ case (meaning highly embellished)
classical music programming (as opposed to popular music)
a romantic setting (meaning romance-inspiring)

7.2.6. Modes. Names of modes are capitalized.

Dorian   Lydian   Hypoaeolian
Hypodorian   Mixolydian   Ionian
Phrygian   Hypomixolydian   Hypoionian
Hypophrygian   Aeolian

7.3. Diacritical marks

7.3.1. Retain. Diacritical marks should be retained; to omit them amounts to misspelling—or, more accurately, mispronouncing—a word. However, many non-English terms with such marks have become so well established in the English language that it is becoming more common to omit the marks. Many dictionaries list both forms of such words. To include diacritical marks, even in English text, is never wrong. Be sure to include any diacritical marks when giving a direct quote.

apropos, à propos	naive, naïve
debut, début	nee, née
deja vu, déjà vu	premiere, première
denouement, dénouement	raison d'etre, raison d'être
elite, élite	role, rôle
facade, façade	voila, voilà

7.3.2. Different words. It is necessary to retain diacritical marks for some words because their exclusion forms a different word.

chargé (diplomatic official) *vs.* charge (responsibility; debt; attack)
exposé (disclosure) *vs.* expose (to lay open)
résumé or resumé (summary) *vs.* resume (to continue)

7.3.3. Musical terms. Generally, non-English musical terms and titles retain their diacritical marks.

agréments	*entrée*	*Má Vlast*
Boléro	étude	*Les Préludes*
bourrée	flûte à bec	*style brisé*
Clavier-Übung	habañera	*Tannhaüser*
détaché	ländler	*Die Zauberflöte*

7.4. Plurals of non-English words

7.4.1. Introduction. Since many musical terms are non-English, there is the question of whether the plural of such terms should be formed as in the original language or anglicized. There is no problem if the plural of a non-English word is formed as in English by simply adding an *s* (such as the French *ouverture, ouvertures*). However, there are many irregular plural forms, and the use of a great number of Italian words—which do not use the letter *s* for plurals—means this matter needs to be addressed. One of the principles of this guide is that even when non-English words are being used in an English context, they should (in most respects) be subject to the rules of English. This is supported by the fact that many anglicized plurals may be found in English dictionaries, such as "arpeggios" and "festschrifts." The decision to use an anglicized plural may have to be based on whether such a format offends the writer's sensibility, or whether the writer believes it may offend the reader's sensibility. Alerting the reader to the use of an anglicized plural is always appropriate.

7.4.2. Italian -*o*. The plural of a single Italian word ending in *o* is formed by changing the *o* to an *i*. (In the accompanying list, "arpeggio" is the exception.) For the anglicized plural form, simply add an *s*. While some original plurals are often seen (concerti), some are rare (arpeggi). Either may be used, but give preference to the anglicized version.

Word	*Original*	*Anglicized*
arpeggio	arpeggi	arpeggios
cello	celli	cellos
concerto	concerti	concertos
libretto	libretti	librettos
ostinato	ostinati	ostinatos
ritornello	ritornelli	ritornellos
stretto	stretti	strettos
tempo	tempi	tempos
virtuoso	virtuosi	virtuosos

7.4.3. Italian -*a*. The plural of a single Italian word ending in *a* is formed by changing the *a* to an *e*. For the anglicized plural form, simply add an *s*. In the following list, the anglicized plurals are usually seen more often in an English context than the originals.

Word	*Original*	*Anglicized*
partita	partite	partitas
sonata	sonate	sonatas
sinfonia	sinfonie	sinfonias
toccata	toccate	toccatas

7.4.4. German. German words with a variety of plural endings may be anglicized with just an *s*. Note that the use of lowercase for the anglicized plurals is a further sign of an assimilated word.

Word	Original	Anglicized
Festschrift	Festschriften	festschrifts
Lied	Lieder	lieds
Rohrflöte	Rohrflöten	rohrflötes
Singspiel	Singspiele	singspiels

7.4.5. French. French words usually add an *s* to form the plural, and so the anglicized plural would be the same. However, there are other plural forms as well as exceptions.

Word	Original	Anglicized
ballade	ballades	ballades
bourrée	bourrées	bourrées
chanson	chansons	chansons
ouverture	ouvertures	ouvertures
rondeau	rondeaux	(rondeaus)
	(by analogy with "bureau / bureaus")	
hautbois	hautbois	——
voix	voix	——

7.4.6. Latin. Latin names may also be anglicized by analogy with other assimilated words. Note that the plural of "cantus" is unchanged. While some anglicized plurals of Latin words have gained wide use— "symposiums," "formulas"—some writers may consider plurals such as "opuses" and "cantuses" unacceptable.

Word	Original	Anglicized
bicinium	bicinia	biciniums
	(by analogy with "symposium / symposiums")	
clausula	clausulae	clausulas
figura	figurae	figuras
	(by analogy with "formula / formulas")	
opus	opera	(opuses)
ordo	ordines	ordos
cantus	cantus	(cantuses)

7.4.7. Greek. Greek terms also have some difficult anglicized plurals.

Word	Original	Anglicized
apotomē	apotomai	apotomes
aulos	auloi	(auloses)
comma	commata	commas
	(This is the interval, not the punctuation mark.)	
melisma	melismata	melismas
nomos	nomoi	(nomoses)
syrinx	syringes	syrinxes
tonos	tonoi	(tonoses)

7.4.8. Unique anglicized plurals. As is evident from the discussion above, there are problems forming anglicized plurals when dealing with some single non-English words with unique plurals, as well as with many compound non-English words. Some examples are shown here.

Word	Original Plural
aulos	auloi
rondeau	rondeaux
cantus firmus	cantus firmi
concerto grosso	concerti grossi
opera buffa	opere buffe
opéra comique	opéras comiques
sinfonia concertante	sinfonie concertanti
port de voix	ports de voix
viola da gamba	viole da gamba

There are many considerations in determining anglicized plurals for these terms. Plurals in English are formed differently than plurals in other languages. For example, many languages pluralize both the noun and its modifier (opere buffe, opéras comiques) whereas in English, the modifier is singular (comic operas). In English, even plural phrases in other contexts become singular when modifying a noun; for example, "pianos that are six feet long" becomes "the six-foot-long pianos." So, an anglicized plural that adds an *s* only to the main word would produce "operas buffa" and "opéras comique." Unfortunately, such forms would look like misspellings to someone familiar with the original language. On the other hand, many compound words in English that identify single concepts and have no main word simply put the *s* at the end, such as "composer-performers." This would produce such anglicized plurals as "opera buffas." (This is related to the growing popular usage of terms such as "sons-in-law" being slowly transformed into "son-in-laws.") But simply adding an *s* on the end to form "opéra comiques" would, again, look like a misspelling. A further complication is that some non-English words have the same spelling for both singular and plural forms, such as the Latin "cantus" and the French "voix." As a result of all these difficulties, one may find that certain compound words have several plurals listed in some English-language dictionaries; for example, for "opera buffa," *Webster's New Universal Unabridged Dictionary* gives three plurals: "operas buffa," "opera buffas," and the original "opere buffe." To deal with these circumstances, the following suggestions are offered.

1. Use the non-English plural, but introduce the term in the singular form first, then alert the reader to the plural form in parentheses.

The aulos (plural: auloi) was a wind instrument of ancient
    Greece. Auloi were . . .
The term *cantus* (Latin, "song," "melody"; plural: *cantus*) is used . .
The earliest type of instrumental concerto in the middle
    and late Baroque period was the concerto grosso
    (plural: concerti grossi). Concerti grossi are . . .

2. Mention the original non-English plural, but inform the reader that an anglicized plural will be used. If the plural is an anglicized one that the reader will not have trouble with, there is no need to specifically announce that plural.

First, we will give a short history of the partita. (The original
    plural is *partite*, but the anglicized form *partitas* is used here.)
A comma is a small difference between two intervals. There
    are several kinds of commas . . .

3. Create a "specialized plural" by taking the singular form of the term and adding a center dot and an *s* (·s). This method is unusual and unconventional, so it should be explained to the reader. It has several advantages: it shows the well-known singular form, it uses the English convention of forming plurals by simply adding a final *s*, it provides a visual distinction between the non-English term and the English plural, and it bypasses the question of *s* versus *es*. This method may work better for some words than others. (Do not use an apostrophe and an *s* ('s) to form a plural of a word.)

cantus·s	opera buffa·s
figura·s	opéra comique·s
rondeau·s	port de voix·s
cantus firmus·s	sinfonia concertante·s
concerto grosso·s	viola da gamba·s

4. Use the term only in the singular if the wording is not too tortuous.

not
Mozart wrote several *opere buffe*.
but
Mozart wrote more than one *opera buffa*.
not
The museum has three viole da gamba.
but
The museum has three examples of the viola da gamba.
not
The soprano demonstrated several *ports de voix*.
but
The soprano demonstrated the *port de voix* several times.

5. Use an English approximation of the term, providing the meaning is properly conveyed. Inform the reader of the original and its approximation at its first mention. Then the translation may be used thereafter. Some terms may be untranslatable either because the term itself has taken on a life of its own and cannot be approximated with an English equivalent, or because a literal translation is unacceptable.

Original Plural	*English Approximation*
bicinia	two-voice compositions
cantus firmi	established melodies
figurae	figurations; note patterns
opere buffe	comic operas
pièces croisées	cross-hand pieces
Rohrflöten	chimney flutes

The *Orgelbüchlein* demonstrates the process of composition
    by note patterns (*figurae*). Such note patterns are . . .
F. Couperin wrote many *pièces croisées* or "cross-hand pieces."
    These cross-hand pieces are . . .

7.5. Word Usage

7.5.1. Arrangement vs. transcription.
An arrangement is the process of adapting a composition for a medium different from that for which it was originally composed; for example, the arrangement of Bach's cello suites for guitar. The word may also refer to the result of such an adaptation ("she played Segovia's arrangement"). A transcription may refer to (1) the copying of a musical work from one form of notation to another (from tablature to staff notation) or from one layout to another (from separate parts to full score); or (2) the transfer of music from a live performance to written notation. One implication of the two terms is that an arrangement is not as strict as a transcription, with the former sometimes involving modification of the original. However, in common usage, the two words are sometimes used interchangeably.

7.5.2. Cello.
The word "cello" is a shortened form of the word "violoncello" and is sometimes written with an apostrophe ('cello). It is suggested that "cello" without an apostrophe be used in an English context. The English form of the plural would then be "cellos." Occasionally one will see the plural as "celli" but this is the Italian form. Some dictionaries give the plural form as "cello" (one cello, two cello); again, "cellos" is recommended.

7.5.3. Chord vs. triad.
A chord is a group of three or more pitches sounding simultaneously. (Some references say two or more pitches.) A triad is a chord of three pitches, with adjacent pitches forming intervals of a third when the triad is in root position. All triads are chords, but not all chords are triads. The most common triads are major (C-E-G), minor (C-E♭-G), augmented (C-E-G♯), and diminished (C-E♭-G♭). Note the arrangement of major and minor thirds. In contrast, a chord may have pitches of C-F-B♭, D-E♭-G, G-A-B-D, and so on.

7.5.4. Disc vs. disk.
The word "disk" is the standard word in United States English for a thin, flat, circular item. The same item in British English is spelled "disc." Today in United States English, "disc" is used to refer to a phonograph record or a compact disc, while "disk" refers to computer-related storage devices such as a floppy disk or a hard disk (hard drive). Technical writers make the distinction that "disk" refers to a magnetic storage medium while "disc" refers to an optical storage medium. Be careful not to refer to a "DVD disc" or a "CD disc" since the final D in each of those terms already stands for "disc."

7.5.5. Frequency vs. pitch. "Frequency" refers to the number of periodic vibrations in a musical tone expressed in cycles per second or hertz (Hz). "Pitch" refers to the subjective experience of frequency as it relates to the highness or lowness of a musical tone; generally, the greater the frequency, the higher the perceived pitch. "Pitch" also refers to a frequency associated with a note name; that is, "440 Hz" is a frequency, "a^l" is a note name, and "$a^l = 440$ Hz" is a pitch.

7.5.6. Historic vs. historical. The word "historical" refers simply to anything that occurred in the past. The word "historic" refers to what is momentous or important from the past.

The museum has eight historical violins.
The museum's Stradivarius violin is a historic instrument.

7.5.7. Key vs. key signature. The word "key" refers to the pitch relationships that establish a single pitch class as a tonal center, such as "Beethoven's Symphony no. 5 is in the key of C minor." The term "key signature" refers to an arrangement of sharps or flats (or the absence of both) at the beginning of each staff, such as "the key signature of C minor has three flats." Thus, "key signature" is an element of notation; "key" is not. Because the word "key" also refers to other musical elements—the individual levers of a keyboard, the levers on a wind-blown instrument—as well as having non-musical meanings ("a thing that explains something" and "essential"), it may be useful in some circumstances to use the word "key signature" in place of simply "key" for clarity.

Playing the natural keys from C to C on a keyboard is an
        example of a diatonic scale in a major key signature.

7.5.8. Ligatures. The ligatures æ (*a* + *e*) and œ (*o* + *e*) are omitted in English transliterated or assimilated words that were originally Latin or Greek. Ligatures are retained in Old English or French words used in their respective contexts, and also retained if in quoted material.

aesthetic, *not* æsthetic
encyclopedia *or* encyclopaedia, *not* encyclopædia
oeuvre, *not* œuvre (as in "a discussion of Bach's oeuvre")
but
œuvres complètes

7.5.9. Measure vs. bar. The word "measure" refers to the recurring element of music notation demarcated by two vertical lines on a staff or staves. The word "bar" is often used synonymously but is more correctly the British term for "measure." The vertical lines that demarcate measures are "bar lines" but are often referred to colloquially as "bars." In United States English, the preferred terms are "measure" and "bar line."

7.5.10. Music vs. musical. The noun "music" and the adjective "musical" are often used to form compound words. (By such compound words is not meant types of music such as "chamber music" or "electronic music" nor to a description of something melodious such as "the musical quality of her voice.") The question arises as to which word should be used in which circumstance. One starting point is the dictionary definitions. The noun "music" is defined in *Webster's New World Dictionary* as (1) the art and science of combining vocal or instrumental sounds or tones in varying melody, harmony, rhythm, and timbre, especially so as to form structurally complete and emotionally expressive compositions; (2) the sounds or tones so arranged; or (3) the written or printed score of a musical composition. The adjective "musical" is defined in *Webster's New World Dictionary* as (1) of or for the creation, production, or performance of music; (2) having the nature of music (melodious or harmonious); (3) fond of, sensitive to, or skilled in music; or (4) set to or accompanied by music. One may need to be guided by how the term "reads" in context. Rewriting a sentence may also clarify a term's function. The following list is given as an illustration of typical word usage of these two terms.

music box	musical acoustics
music conference	musical clock
music education	musical comedy
music festival	musical composition
music genre	musical instrument
music hall	musical notation
music history	musical performance
music publisher	musical play
music school	musical structure
music teacher	musical style
music theory	musical term
music therapy	musical theater

7.5.11. Note vs. tone. A "note" is a symbol used in musical notation that represents a single sound with a particular duration and—when placed on a staff—pitch (whole note, quarter note). The term is also used to refer to the sound or pitch itself (as in "the oboist played a wrong note"). The term "tone" has several different meanings: (1) the interval of two semitones; that is, a whole tone or major second; (2) any steady sound, especially one used in making measurements (pure tone, test tone); (3) the quality of a musical sound (nasal tone; flutey tone); and (4) the United States English word for "note" or "pitch."

7.5.12. Opus and opera. The word "opus" is the Latin word for "work," used in a musical context to mean a musical composition. It is usually used in its abbreviated form "op." with a number as an identifier. Occasionally the word is written out if it is the first word in a sentence, if the subject of opus numbers is being discussed, or sometimes—but not always—if it is the only identifier to a work, as in "Beethoven's Symphony opus 67." The plural of "opus" is "opera" (abbreviated "opp.") which is seen in such references as "Chopin's Études opp. 10 and 25." An anglicized plural of "opus" is "opuses," which is not universally accepted. The word "opera" also refers to the theatrical genre in which the text is primarily sung. Several suggestions for the use of these words are: (1) use "opera" only for the genre; (2) use the abbreviations "op." and "opp."—not the written-out words—as identifiers; (3) do not use the word "opus" in running text when the words "composition," "piece," or "work" will do; and (4) break the above three rules only when the meaning can be made absolutely clear to the reader.

7.5.13. Piano vs. pianoforte vs. fortepiano. The word "piano" is the accepted modern term for the stringed keyboard instrument with felt hammers. The word "pianoforte" is another term for the same instrument, although the word is rather outmoded in United States English. The word "fortepiano" is sometimes used to refer to an early form of the piano found in the eighteenth and early nineteenth centuries.

7.5.14. Record vs. recording. A "record" in a musical context refers to the thin, flat, circular grooved item played on a phonograph. The noun "recording" is in one respect a synonym for "record," but some writers prefer to use the word "recording" to refer to the process of making a record. Other writers bypass the problem and use the terms "33 rpm disc" and "45 rpm disc" in place of "record" as a means of uniformity with the term "compact disc." The term "sound recording" may be used as a general term to mean any of the various ways of capturing aural material for playback. The word "album" is a carry-over from 78 rpm records which were contained in book-like folders; so "album" is short for "record album" and may be considered a synonym for "record."

7.5.15. Uniform titles. Although some genres have different spellings based on different national styles, it is necessary for general writing purposes to select one spelling or form to stand for the entire genre; for example, "allemande" instead of "alemana," "allemand," "allemanda," "almain," or "almand." This is referred to as a *uniform title*. The exceptions to this are when one is quoting the exact title of a piece, discussing a specific national style, or emphasizing the differences in national styles. Suggested uniform titles are listed below.

allemande	gavotte	overture	quintet
bagatelle	gigue	partita	recitative
barcarolle	invention	passacaglia	sarabande
bourrée	march	pastorale	siciliana
chaconne	minuet	postlude	sonata
courante	motet	prelude	symphony
galliard	nocturne	quartet	waltz

but
the Almand from Purcell's Suite no. 1
Bach's Partia, BWV 1002 (to use the composer's term)
the differences between the French *courante* and the
    Italian *corrente*

While written in a gentle 6/8 meter and centered around the key of D major, there are several elements of the harmony that disrupt that gentleness, such as the fluctuation between F-sharp and F-natural, and modulation to remote keys later.

8

Citations

8.1. Introduction. This chapter discusses several types of specialty reference material that would be documented in a musical context. The two methods of documenting material—the author-date system and the notes-and-bibliography system—are equally accepted. The latter will be described here. If one chooses to use the author-date system instead, it is not difficult to convert the formats presented here to that method, since the same documentation is present in both, just arranged differently.

8.2. Printed material

8.2.1 Music editions or scores. The composer's name is given as the "author." If available, the publisher's catalog number should also be included. If the edition is a reprint or a facsimile, this should be noted. (N = notes, B = bibliography)

N: 1. Tori Amos, *Little Earthquakes*, AM 90041
(New York: Amsco Publications, 1992).

B: Amos, Tori. *Little Earthquakes*. AM 90041.
New York: Amsco Publications, 1992.

N: 2. Johann Sebastian Bach, *The Six French Suites*,
ed. Alfred Dürr, BA 5166 (Kassel: Bärenreiter, 1984).

B: Bach, Johann Sebastian. *The Six French Suites*. Edited
by Alfred Dürr. BA 5166. Kassel: Bärenreiter, 1984.

N: 3. Jean-Philippe Rameau, *Complete Works for Solo
Keyboard* (Reprint, New York: Dover Publications, 1993).

B: Rameau, Jean-Philippe. *Complete Works for Solo Keyboard*.
Reprint, New York: Dover Publications, 1993.

8.2.2. Notes to music editions or scores. This refers to the text included with a music edition, such as editorial and/or commentary material. It may or may not have its own title.

N: 4. Wolfgang Plath and Wolfgang Rehm, "Preface,"
           translated by Faye Ferguson, in Wolfgang Amadeus
           Mozart, *Piano Sonatas*, 2 vols., ed. Wolfgang Plath
           and Wolfgang Rehm. BA 4861b, BA 4862b
           (Kassel: Bärenreiter, 1986).

B: Plath, Wolfgang and Wolfgang Rehm. "Preface."
           Translated by Faye Ferguson. In Wolfgang Amadeus
           Mozart, *Piano Sonatas*, 2 vols. Edited by Wolfgang
           Plath and Wolfgang Rehm. BA 4861b, BA 4862b.
           Kassel: Bärenreiter, 1986.

N: 5. Peter Williams, notes for *G. F. Handel, Organ
           Concerto in F major, Op. 4, No. 5*, ed. Peter Williams.
           EE 6676 (London: Eulenburg, 1978).

B: Williams, Peter. Notes for *G. F. Handel, Organ Concerto
           in F major, Op. 4, No. 5*. Edited by Peter Williams.
           EE 6676. London: Eulenburg, 1978.

8.2.3. Texts accompanying recordings. As with prefatory material to a music edition, texts with a recording (traditionally called "liner notes") and program notes to a concert may or may not have their own title. Observe that the title of the notes is in quotation marks and the title of the recording is in italics.

N: 6. Gregory Fulkerson, "The Unaccompanied
           Sonatas and Partitas of J. S. Bach," liner notes for
           *J. S. Bach: The Sonatas and Partitas for
           Unaccompanied Violin*, Gregory Fulkerson, violin.
           2 CDs (Bridge Records 9101A/B, 2000).

B: Fulkerson, Gregory. "The Unaccompanied Sonatas and
           Partitas of J. S. Bach." Liner notes for *J. S. Bach:
           The Sonatas and Partitas for Unaccompanied Violin*,
           Gregory Fulkerson, violin. 2 CDs. Bridge Records
           9101A/B, 2000.

N: 7. Richard Drakeford, liner notes for *A Warlock Centenary Album*, CD (EMI Classics 7243 5 65101 2 8, 1994).

B: Drakeford, Richard. Liner notes for *A Warlock Centenary Album*. CD. EMI Classics 7243 5 65101 2 8, 1994.

8.2.4. Program notes

N: 8. Thomas Donahue, program notes for *A Concert in Honor of Johann Sebastian Bach* (Willard Memorial Chapel, Auburn, New York, 21 March 1993).

B: Donahue, Thomas. Program notes for *A Concert in Honor of Johann Sebastian Bach*. Willard Memorial Chapel, Auburn, New York, 21 March 1993.

8.3. Audiovisual material

8.3.1 Sound recordings. The information provided on sound recordings does not tend to be as uniform as that for books. The information for a recording should include the composer, the title(s) of the piece(s), either the performer and the instrument, or the ensemble and the conductor, the medium (long-playing record, cassette, compact disc, Web download), the record company, the catalog number, and the year. If there is a unique title for the recording, include that also (*Horowitz on Television*, *A Warlock Centenary Album*). While the lead item for documenting a book is usually the author, for a sound recording it may be the unique title, the composer, the performer, the performing ensemble, or the conductor. One needs to make a decision as to which item takes priority. This may vary for different circumstances; for example, a given recording may be listed under either the composer or the performer depending on the focus of the essay at hand. It may be necessary to arrange or reword the information given on the recording, because (1) it may be given in a format unsuited to documentation; (2) the information may be incomplete; and (3) there may be different formats for the front cover, back cover, liner notes, and on the disc or record itself. Sometimes information may be omitted; a discography of Glenn Gould would not need the phrase "Glenn Gould, piano" included in every citation. To supply additional information beyond the basics given above depends on the reason for the citation; for example, in an anthology, listing all composers and all titles. If a large amount of

additional information is to be given, consider including it as an anno-
tation. Recordings are not listed in the bibliography but in a separate
discography. (D = discography)

N: 9. *Horowitz on Television.* Vladimir Horowitz, piano.
LP (Columbia MS 7106, 1968).

D: *Horowitz on Television.* Vladimir Horowitz, piano.
LP. Columbia MS 7106, 1968.

N: 10. Israel Kamakawiwoʻole, *Facing Future.* CD
(Bigboy BBCD 5901, 1993).

D: Kamakawiwoʻole, Israel. *Facing Future.* CD. Bigboy
BBCD 5901, 1993.

N: 11. Wolfgang Amadeus Mozart, *Symphonies Nos. 38
and 39.* The Academy of Ancient Music, directed by
Christopher Hogwood. CD (L'Oiseau-Lyre 410 233-2,
1983, 1984).

D: Mozart, Wolfgang Amadeus. *Symphonies Nos. 38 and
39.* The Academy of Ancient Music, directed by
Christopher Hogwood. CD. L'Oiseau-Lyre 410 233-2,
1983, 1984.

8.3.2 Video recordings
(V = videography)

N: 12. *Castles of the Soul: The Pipe Organs of Gerhard
Brunzema.* VHS (Kitchener, Ontario, Canada: A Rogers
Community 20 Production, 1991).

V: *Castles of the Soul: The Pipe Organs of Gerhard
Brunzema.* VHS. Kitchener, Ontario, Canada:
A Rogers Community 20 Production, 1991.

N: 13. Phil Collins, *Live and Loose in Paris.* DVD (Image
Entertainment ID0080WIDVD, 1997).

V: Collins, Phil. *Live and Loose in Paris.* DVD. Image
Entertainment ID0080WIDVD, 1997.

8.3.3. Television and radio broadcasts. Notice that the name of the program is in roman and quotation marks while the program series is in italics.

N: 14. "Corrette's Christmas Symphonies," *In Concert* (EWTN, 24 December 2006).

B: "Corrette's Christmas Symphonies." *In Concert.* EWTN, 24 December 2006.

N: 15. "An Organist's Yearbook," *Pipedreams*, program no. 0652 (American Public Media, 24 December 2006).

B: "An Organist's Yearbook." *Pipedreams*, program no. 0652. American Public Media, 24 December 2006.

8.3.4. Live performances. If the program lists a title for the concert, place that title first; otherwise use a generic title such as "Concert" or "Recital." If there is a unique title for the concert, it may be set off by the use of italics.

N: 16. Concert, Pinchas Zukerman, violin, The New York Philharmonic, Zubin Mehta, conductor (New York, 6 January 2007).

B: Concert, Pinchas Zukerman, violin, The New York Philharmonic, Zubin Mehta, conductor. New York, 6 January 2007.

N: 17. Concert of Music for Guitar, Keawala'i Congregational Church, Makena, Maui, 16 August 2007.

B: Concert of Music for Guitar. Keawala'i Congregational Church, Makena, Maui, 16 August 2007.

N: 18. *Tiffany Reflections.* Auburn Chamber Orchestra, Ubaldo Valli, conductor (Willard Memorial Chapel, Auburn, New York, 4 March 2005).

B: *Tiffany Reflections.* Auburn Chamber Orchestra, Ubaldo Valli, conductor. Willard Memorial Chapel, Auburn, New York, 4 March 2005.

8.3.5. World Wide Web material. The Web may also be a source for sound recordings, video recordings, archived broadcasts, and live performances. The difficulty with the Web is that internet addresses and their content are constantly being updated, changed, or removed at a fast rate. For this reason, it is not advisable to rely heavily on Web documentation unless absolutely necessary. Try to identify the origin of the material (such as the original recording from which a sound file was taken) or try to find an alternate source of documentation.

N: 19. Andrés Segovia, Master Class, Spain, 1965. Video.
         http://www.youtube.com/watch?v=CNjNXuGQaAE
         (accessed 7 September 2009).

B: Segovia, Andrés. Master Class, Spain, 1965. Video.
         http://www.youtube.com/watch?v=CNjNXuGQaAE
         (accessed 7 September 2009).

8.4. Physical artifacts

8.4.1. Original or unpublished manuscripts. Use the same format as a published score, but substitute the owner or the location in place of the publisher, and, if in a library, include the reference number.

N: 20. John Challis, J. S. Bach's Chaconne in D minor,
         BWV 1004, arranged for harpsichord (Music Division,
         Library of Congress: ML 96.5.C5 case).

B: Challis, John. J. S. Bach's Chaconne in D minor,
         BWV 1004, arranged for harpsichord. Music Division,
         Library of Congress: ML 96.5.C5 case.

8.4.2. Musical instruments. For musical instruments, the maker is the "author." If the maker is unknown, use either "Anonymous" or list the instrument by type. Instruments that are privately owned may not be able to be thoroughly documented if the owner requests that some information be withheld.

N: 21. Pascal Taskin, Two-Manual Harpsichord. Paris,
         1769. (Edinburgh: Edinburgh University Collection of
         Historic Musical Instruments HD7-PT1769.15).

B: Taskin, Pascal. Two-Manual Harpsichord. Paris, 1769.
      Edinburgh: Edinburgh University Collection of
      Historic Musical Instruments HD7-PT1769.15.

N: 22. Anonymous, Transverse Flute (France, ca. eighteenth
      century, private collection).

B: Anonymous. Transverse Flute. France, ca. eighteenth
          century. Private collection.
      or
      Flute, Transverse. France, ca. eighteenth century.
      Private collection.

8.4.3. Drawings. For a technical drawing of a musical instrument, the
person who did the drawing is the "author." The name of the maker of
the instrument and the description of the instrument are both incorporated into the title of the drawing.

N: 23. Richard Loucks, *Fretted Clavichord, Christian
      Gottlob Hubert, Ansbach, 1784.* (Edinburgh:
      Edinburgh University Collection of Historic Musical
      Instruments C4-CH1784.38. Drawing, 1974, 1977, 1981.)

B: Loucks, Richard. *Fretted Clavichord, Christian Gottlob
          Hubert, Ansbach, 1784.* Edinburgh: Edinburgh
      University Collection of Historic Musical Instruments
      C4-CH1784.38. Drawing, 1974, 1977, 1981.

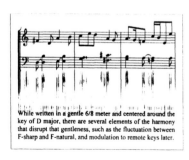

While written in a gentle 6/8 meter and centered around the
key of D major, there are several elements of the harmony
that disrupt that gentleness, such as the fluctuation between
F-sharp and F-natural, and modulation to remote keys later.

Glossary of Typographic Terms

arabic numerals. The figures 0, 1, 2, 3, 4, 5, 6, 7, 8, and 9. Cf. **roman numerals.**

baseline. The imaginary horizontal line on which a line of letters rest; that is: _____ . The descending portion of letters such as *g* and *p* extend below the baseline.

boldface. Refers to letters whose appearance is darker and thicker than regular letters. **This is boldface type.** Cf. *italic type.*

capital letter. The form of a letter used as the first letter of the first word of a sentence, or as the first letter of a proper noun; that is, A, B, C, D, E, and so on, as opposed to a, b, c, d, e. Capital letters are characterized by their uniform height, with the exception of the letter Q and sometimes J which extend below the baseline.

capitalization. A word that is capitalized has its first letter as a capital letter, and all other letters are lowercase; for example, January, Brooklyn, Debussy. This is sometimes called "capitals and lowercase" in contrast to "small caps" WHICH LOOKS LIKE THIS, "caps and small caps" WHICH LOOKS LIKE THIS, and "all caps" WHICH LOOKS LIKE THIS.

cardinal number. Any number used in counting or for showing how many: one, two, three, four, and so on. Cf. **ordinal number.**

compound word. A combination of two or more words or word components that convey a single idea or concept. A compound word may be open ("lower case"), hyphenated ("lower-case"), or closed ("lowercase"). Another term for "closed" is "solid."

diacritical mark, diacritic. A mark added to a letter to indicate a pronunciation different from the unmarked letter. Examples include acute accent (é), cedilla (ç), circumflex (ê), grave accent (è), tilde (ñ), and umlaut (ü).

em dash. A short elevated horizontal line traditionally defined as the length of an uppercase M (—) but more properly defined as the length of the current point size; that is, in twelve-point type, an em dash is twelve points long. (A point is 1/72 inch.)

en dash. A short elevated horizontal line traditionally defined as the length of an uppercase N (–) but more properly defined as one-half the length of an em dash.

font. A complete assortment of type in one size and style. For example, Palatino is a typeface, 12-point Palatino Roman is one font, 10-point Palatino Roman is another font, 10-point Palatino Italic is yet another. Commonly, "font" is sometimes used as a synonym for "typeface." While there is a strict distinction between the two terms, usually this distinction is made only by professional typographers. Cf. **typeface**.

headline style. A style of capitalization in which the first word and all principal words are capitalized, while articles, conjunctions, and most prepositions are lowercase; for example, *The Art of Capitalization: How to Use Letters with Simon's Method*. Cf. **sentence style**.

house style. The collective guidelines and rules for writing suggested or preferred by a publisher, periodical, or organization, which describe word usage, typography, punctuation, and so on.

italics, italic type. Letters that are slanted upward to the right, resembling cursive writing. Italic letters are based on an ellipse rather than a circle. *This is italic type*.

justification. The process of spacing full lines of text so that they are the same length, and so the left and right margins are straight, even, aligned, or flush.

Latin alphabet. A collection of letters (A, B, C, D, etc.) used for the languages of Latin, English, French, Italian, and so on, as opposed to the languages of Chinese, Hebrew, Russian, and so on.

ligature. Two characters "tied" together to form a single character; for example, æ (*a* + *e*) and œ (*o* + *e*).

lowercase. Pertaining to letter forms that are not capitalized; that is, a, b, c, d, e, as opposed to A, B, C, D, E. Lowercase letters are not all the same height, having letters with ascenders (b, d, f, h, k, l, t) and descenders (g, j, p, q, y). Cf. **uppercase**.

ordinal number. Any number used to indicate degree, quality, or position in a series: first, second, third, fourth, and so on. Cf. **cardinal number**.

proper. Designating a name, noun, or adjective that refers to a specific person, place, or thing. In English, proper words have their first letters capitalized: British, Brooklyn Bridge, Iceland, Phoebe.

punctuation. 1. The use of non-letter characters such as a period, comma, colon, semicolon, etc., in order to clarify the meaning of written sentences. 2. The characters themselves, more properly called punctuation marks.

readability. The property of something written—based on its format, grammar, punctuation, syntax, and word usage—that governs the ease with which its meaning may be perceived and understood.

roman numerals. Letters used to represent numbers: I = 1, V = 5, X = 10, L = 50, C = 100, D = 500, M = 1000. While usually uppercase, lowercase roman numerals are sometimes used; for example, as page numbers in the front matter of a book. Cf. **arabic numerals.**

roman type. Letters that stand upright or have a strong vertical emphasis. This is roman type. Cf. **italic type.**

running text. Words arranged in sentences and paragraphs, as opposed to (1) words or phrases arranged in lists, and (2) poetry. Also referred to as narrative text, prose, or body text.

sentence style. A style of capitalization in which the only words that are capitalized are the first word, the first word in a subtitle, and any proper words; for example, *The art of capitalization: How to use letters with Simon's method.* Cf. **headline style.**

small capital letters, small caps. Capital letter forms that do not rise as high as regular capital letters. THESE ARE SMALL CAPITAL LETTERS, while THESE ARE REGULAR CAPITAL LETTERS.

subscript. A figure, letter, or symbol placed below and to the side of another. With the term C_4, 4 is a subscript.

superscript. A figure, letter, or symbol placed above and to the side of another. With the term c^2, 2 is a superscript.

transliteration. The process of writing or spelling words in corresponding letters of another alphabet; in the present context, it refers to the conversion to the Latin alphabet of words from languages that do not use the Latin alphabet, such as Greek, Hebrew, Russian, and so on. For example, the Russian name Стравинский may be transliterated as "Stravinskij."

typeface. Any design of the full range of characters such as letters, numbers, and punctuation marks, in a variety of sizes. Typefaces include Baskerville, Garamond, Palatino, and so on. Cf. **font.**

typography. 1. The arrangement, style, appearance, etc., of material printed with type. 2. The art or process of printing with type.

uppercase. Pertaining to letter forms that are capitalized; that is, A, B, C, D, E, as opposed to a, b, c, d, e. Cf. **lowercase.**

word division. The separation of a multi-syllabic word between syllables, done at the end of a line of text by means of a hyphen, for the purpose of evenly spacing letters and words. Also referred to as end-line hyphenation.

Bibliography

Style Guides

Bellman, Jonathan. *A Short Guide to Writing about Music*. New York: Longman, 2000.

Cambridge University Press. *Instructions for Contributors: Eighteenth-Century Music*, n.d. http://assets.cambridge.org/ECM/ECM_ifc.pdf (accessed 10 November 2006).

Cassaro, James P., et al. *Notes Style Sheet*. Music Library Association, 2006. http://www.areditions.com/mla/notes/stylesheet.html (accessed 21 October 2006).

The Chicago Manual of Style, 15th ed. Chicago: University of Chicago Press, 2003.

Cowdery, James R., ed. *How to Write about Music: The RILM Manual of Style*. 2nd ed. New York: Répertoire Internationale de Littérature Musicale, 2006.

Helm, E. Eugene, and Albert T. Luper. *Words and Music: Form and Procedure in Theses, Dissertations, Research Papers, Book Reports, Programs, Theses in Composition*. Rev. ed. Totowa, N.J.: European American Music Corporation, 1982.

Herbert, Trevor. *Music in Words: A Guide to Researching and Writing about Music*. London: The Associated Board of the Royal Schools of Music, 2001.

Holoman, D. Kern. *Writing about Music: A Style Sheet from the Editors of 19th-Century Music*. Berkeley: University of California Press, 1988.

Irvine, Demar. *Irvine's Writing about Music*. 3rd ed. Rev. and enlarged by Mark A. Radice. Portland, Ore.: Amadeus Press, 1999.

Strunk, William, Jr., and E. B. White. *The Elements of Style*. New York: Macmillan, 1959.

Style Guide. Chicago: Northwestern University School of Music, 2006. http://www.music.northwestern.edu/pdf/faculty/SOMStyleGuide.pdf (accessed 19 October 2006).

Style Guide for Editors and Proofreaders of IDRC Books. Ottawa, Canada: The International Development Research Centre, 2003. http://archive.idrc.ca/books/edit/eindex.html (accessed 29 November 2006).

Style Sheet. Journal of Seventeenth-Century Music, 2006. http://www.sscm-jscm.org (accessed 19 September 2006).

United States Government Printing Office Style Manual. Washington, D.C.: Government Printing Office, 2000. http://www.gpoaccess.gov/stylemanual/browse.html (accessed 27 November 2006).

Wingell, Richard J. *Writing about Music: An Introductory Guide.* 2nd ed. Upper Saddle River, N.J.: Prentice Hall, 1997.

Wright, Don. *Citing Music Sources in Your Essay and Bibliography.* Rev. and enlarged by Lisa Rae Philpott. University of Western Ontario, 2004. http://www.lib.uwo.ca/music/citemus.html (accessed 21 October 2006).

Writing about Music: An Essay Style Guide. Department of Music, Mount Allison University, 2005. http://www.mta.ca/music/academics/guides/styleguide/index.html (accessed 3 November 2006).

Music References

Boyd, Malcolm, ed. *Oxford Composer Companions: J. S. Bach.* Oxford: Oxford University Press, 1999.

Cross, Milton, and David Ewen. *Milton Cross' Encyclopedia of the Great Composers and Their Music.* 2 vols. Garden City, N.Y.: Doubleday, 1962.

Grout, Donald Jay. *A History of Western Music.* Rev. ed. New York: W. W. Norton, 1973.

Hixon, Donald L. *Music Abbreviations: A Reverse Dictionary.* Lanham, Md.: Scarecrow Press, 2005.

Lloyd, Norman, ed. *The Golden Encyclopedia of Music.* New York: Golden Press, 1968.

Macy, Laura, ed. *Grove Music Online.* http://www.grovemusic.com (accessed September 2005 and November 2006–January 2007).

"Music Dictionary." *Dolmetsch Online.* http://www.dolmetsch.com/musictheorydefs.htm (accessed December 2006–August 2007).

Pronouncing Dictionary of Music and Musicians. 2nd ed. Ames: Iowa State University, 2002. http://www.iowapublicradio.org/dictionary/ (accessed August 2007).

Randel, Don Michael, ed. *The Harvard Biographical Dictionary of Music.* Cambridge, Mass.: The Belknap Press of Harvard University Press, 1996.

Randel, Don Michael, ed. *The New Harvard Dictionary of Music*. Cambridge, Mass.: The Belknap Press of Harvard University Press, 1986.

Dictionaries

Dictionary.com. http://www.dictionary.reference.com/ (accessed December 2006–August 2007).

Merriam-Webster Online. http://www.m-w.com/ (accessed December 2006–August 2007).

Merriam-Webster's Collegiate® Dictionary. 11th ed. Springfield, Mass.: Merriam-Webster, 2003.

OneLook® Dictionary Search. http://www.onelook.com/ (accessed December 2006).

Webster's New Universal Unabridged Dictionary. New York: Barnes & Noble Books, 1989.

Webster's New World Dictionary and Thesaurus. 2nd ed. New York: Hungry Minds, 2002.

Webster's New World Dictionary of the American Language. Second College Edition. New York: World Publishing, 1970.

Webster's Third New International Dictionary, Unabridged. Merriam-Webster, 2002. http://unabridged.merriam-webster.com (accessed September 2007).

Language References

Caldwell, Ann, Jeffrey Earnest, Lynn Gullickson, and Michelle Koth. *Types of Compositions for Use in Music Uniform Titles*, 2002. http://www.library.yale.edu/cataloging/music/types.htm (accessed 7 January 2007).

"Chicago Style Q & A: Capitalization, Titles." *The Chicago Manual of Style Online*. http://www.chicagomanualofstyle.org/CMS_FAQ/CapitalizationTitles/CapitalizationTitles_questions01.html (accessed 26 August 2007).

"English Compound." *Wikipedia*. Wikimedia Foundation, Inc., 2006. http://en.wikipedia.org/wiki/English_compound (accessed 28 November 2006).

Horne, Scott. "Accents and Other Diacritical Marks in English." *Horne Translations*, 2002. http://www.hornetranslations.com/diacriticsenca.html (accessed 2 September 2007).

Keary, Major. "On Hyphenation: Anarchy of Pedantry." *PC Update Online!* 1991. http://www.melbpc.org.au/pcupdate/9100/9112article4.htm (accessed 19 November 2006).

"Language Tools: Capitalization of Key, Opus, and Numbers." *Music Cataloging at Yale*. http://www.library.yale.edu/cataloging/music/musicat.htm (accessed 7 January 2007).

Lawless, Laura K. "Capitalization of French Titles and Names." *About: French Language*. http://french.about.com/library/writing/bl-capitalizationoftitles.htm (accessed 7 January 2007).

Woestenburg, J. C. "*TALŌ's Language Technology: Hyphenators, Spell Checkers, Dictionaries." 7th ed. 2006. http://www.talo.nl/talo/download/documents/Language_Book.pdf (accessed 16 August 2007).

Typographic References

Adobe Systems, Inc. *A Glossary of Typographic Terms*. http://www.adobe.com/type/topics/glossary.html (accessed 14 January 2007).

Callery, Emma. *The Complete Calligrapher. A Comprehensive Guide from Basic Techniques to Inspirational Alphabets*. London: Quantum Books, 2002.

Index

The numbers refer to sections, not pages.

About the Author

Thomas Donahue received his D.D.S. degree from the State University of New York at Buffalo in 1979. He studied piano and organ with Frank Newcomb, organ with George Damp, organ and harpsichord with Anthony Newman (State University of New York at Purchase) and harpsichord with Joyce Lindorff (Cornell University). His articles have appeared in both music periodicals and dental journals. He is the author of *A Guide to Musical Temperament* (Scarecrow, 2005) and the editor of *Gerhard Brunzema: His Work and His Influence* (Scarecrow, 1998), and *Anthony Newman: Music, Energy, Spirit, Healing* (Scarecrow, 2001). When not playing or writing about harpsichords and pipe organs, he enjoys building and restoring them. He lives in New York State with his wife Jane.

Breinigsville, PA USA
18 October 2010
247497BV00004B/2/P